William Shakespeare (bapt. 26 April 1564 – 23 April 1616) was an English poet, playwright and actor, widely regarded as the greatest writer in the English language and the world's greatest dramatist. He is often called England's national poet and the "Bard of Avon". His extant works, including collaborations, consist of approximately 39 plays, 154 sonnets, two long narrative poems, and a few other verses, some of uncertain authorship. His plays have been translated into every major living language and are performed more often than those of any other playwright. Shakespeare was born and raised in Stratford-upon-Avon, Warwickshire. At the age of 18, he married Anne Hathaway, with whom he had three children: Susanna and twins Hamnet and Judith. Sometime between 1585 and 1592, he began a successful career in London as an actor, writer, and part-owner of a playing company called the Lord Chamberlain's Men, later known as the King's Men. At age 49 (around 1613), he appears to have retired to Stratford, where he died three years later. (Source: Wikipedia)

Literary works:
The Tempest
The Two Gentlemen of Verona
The Merry Wives of Windsor
Measure for Measure
The Comedy of Errors
Much Ado About Nothing
Love's Labour's Lost
A Midsummer Night's Dream
The Merchant of Venice
As You Like It
The Taming of the Shrew
All's Well That Ends Well
Twelfth Night
The Winter's Tale
Pericles, Prince of Tyre
The Two Noble Kinsmen

THE TRAGEDY OF OTHELLO,
THE MOOR OF VENICE

William Shakespeare

PRINCE CLASSICS

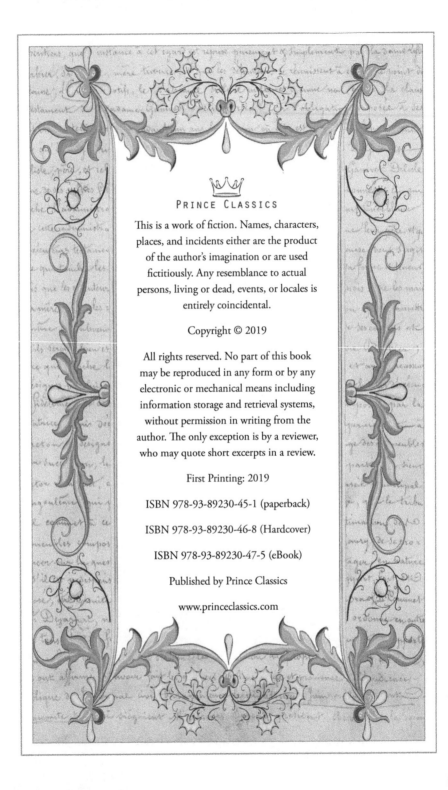

First Printing: 2019

ISBN 978-93-89230-45-1 (paperback)

ISBN 978-93-89230-46-8 (Hardcover)

ISBN 978-93-89230-47-5 (eBook)

Published by Prince Classics

www.princeclassics.com

Contents

Dramatis Personæ   9

ACT I   **11**

SCENE I. Venice. A street.   11

SCENE II. Venice. Another street.   22

SCENE III. Venice. A council chamber.   29

ACT II   **50**

SCENE I. A seaport in Cyprus. A Platform.   50

SCENE II. A street.   67

SCENE III. A Hall in the Castle.   68

ACT III   **88**

SCENE I. Cyprus. Before the Castle.   88

SCENE II. Cyprus. A Room in the Castle.   92

SCENE III. Cyprus. The Garden of the Castle.   93

SCENE IV. Cyprus. Before the Castle.   124

ACT IV   **138**

SCENE I. Cyprus. Before the Castle.   138

SCENE II. Cyprus. A Room in the Castle.   158

SCENE III. Cyprus. Another Room in the Castle.   174

ACT V   **181**

SCENE I. Cyprus. A Street.   181

SCENE II. Cyprus. A Bedchamber in the castle.   192

About Author   221

THE TRAGEDY OF OTHELLO,
THE MOOR OF VENICE

Dramatis Personæ

DUKE OF VENICE

BRABANTIO, a Senator of Venice and Desdemona's father

Other Senators

GRATIANO, Brother to Brabantio

LODOVICO, Kinsman to Brabantio

OTHELLO, a noble Moor in the service of Venice

CASSIO, his Lieutenant

IAGO, his Ancient

MONTANO, Othello's predecessor in the government of Cyprus

RODERIGO, a Venetian Gentleman

CLOWN, Servant to Othello

DESDEMONA, Daughter to Brabantio and Wife to Othello

EMILIA, Wife to Iago

BIANCA, Mistress to Cassio

Officers, Gentlemen, Messenger, Musicians, Herald, Sailor, Attendants, &c.

SCENE: The First Act in Venice; during the rest of the Play at a Seaport in Cyprus.

ACT I

SCENE I. Venice. A street.

Enter Roderigo and Iago.

RODERIGO.

Tush, never tell me, I take it much unkindly

That thou, Iago, who hast had my purse,

As if the strings were thine, shouldst know of this.

IAGO.

'Sblood, but you will not hear me.

If ever I did dream of such a matter,

Abhor me.

RODERIGO.

Thou told'st me, thou didst hold him in thy hate.

IAGO.

Despise me if I do not. Three great ones of the city,

In personal suit to make me his lieutenant,

Off-capp'd to him; and by the faith of man,

I know my price, I am worth no worse a place.

But he, as loving his own pride and purposes,

Evades them, with a bombast circumstance,

Horribly stuff'd with epithets of war:

And in conclusion,

Nonsuits my mediators: for "Certes," says he,

"I have already chose my officer."

And what was he?

Forsooth, a great arithmetician,

One Michael Cassio, a Florentine,

A fellow almost damn'd in a fair wife,

That never set a squadron in the field,

Nor the division of a battle knows

More than a spinster, unless the bookish theoric,

Wherein the toged consuls can propose

As masterly as he: mere prattle without practice

Is all his soldiership. But he, sir, had the election,

And I, of whom his eyes had seen the proof

At Rhodes, at Cyprus, and on other grounds,

Christian and heathen, must be belee'd and calm'd

By debitor and creditor, this counter-caster,

He, in good time, must his lieutenant be,

And I, God bless the mark, his Moorship's ancient.

RODERIGO.

By heaven, I rather would have been his hangman.

IAGO.

Why, there's no remedy. 'Tis the curse of service,

Preferment goes by letter and affection,

And not by old gradation, where each second

Stood heir to the first. Now sir, be judge yourself

Whether I in any just term am affin'd

To love the Moor.

RODERIGO.

I would not follow him, then.

IAGO.

O, sir, content you.

I follow him to serve my turn upon him:

We cannot all be masters, nor all masters

Cannot be truly follow'd. You shall mark

Many a duteous and knee-crooking knave

That, doting on his own obsequious bondage,

Wears out his time, much like his master's ass,

For nought but provender, and when he's old, cashier'd.

Whip me such honest knaves. Others there are

Who, trimm'd in forms, and visages of duty,

Keep yet their hearts attending on themselves,

And throwing but shows of service on their lords,

Do well thrive by them, and when they have lin'd their coats,

Do themselves homage. These fellows have some soul,

And such a one do I profess myself. For, sir,

It is as sure as you are Roderigo,

Were I the Moor, I would not be Iago:

In following him, I follow but myself.

Heaven is my judge, not I for love and duty,

But seeming so for my peculiar end.

For when my outward action doth demonstrate

The native act and figure of my heart

In complement extern, 'tis not long after

But I will wear my heart upon my sleeve

For daws to peck at: I am not what I am.

RODERIGO.

What a full fortune does the thick-lips owe,

If he can carry't thus!

IAGO.

Call up her father,

Rouse him, make after him, poison his delight,

Proclaim him in the streets; incense her kinsmen,

And though he in a fertile climate dwell,

Plague him with flies: though that his joy be joy,

Yet throw such changes of vexation on't,

As it may lose some color.

RODERIGO.

Here is her father's house, I'll call aloud.

IAGO.

Do, with like timorous accent and dire yell

As when, by night and negligence, the fire

Is spied in populous cities.

RODERIGO.

What ho, Brabantio! Signior Brabantio, ho!

IAGO.

Awake! what ho, Brabantio! Thieves, thieves!

Look to your house, your daughter, and your bags!

Thieves, thieves!

Brabantio appears above at a window.

BRABANTIO.

What is the reason of this terrible summons?

What is the matter there?

RODERIGO.

Signior, is all your family within?

IAGO.

Are your doors locked?

BRABANTIO.

Why, wherefore ask you this?

IAGO.

Zounds, sir, you're robb'd, for shame put on your gown,

Your heart is burst, you have lost half your soul;

Even now, now, very now, an old black ram

Is tupping your white ewe. Arise, arise,

Awake the snorting citizens with the bell,

Or else the devil will make a grandsire of you:

Arise, I say.

BRABANTIO.

What, have you lost your wits?

RODERIGO.

Most reverend signior, do you know my voice?

BRABANTIO.

Not I. What are you?

RODERIGO.

My name is Roderigo.

BRABANTIO.

The worser welcome.

I have charg'd thee not to haunt about my doors;

In honest plainness thou hast heard me say

My daughter is not for thee; and now in madness,

Being full of supper and distempering draughts,

Upon malicious bravery, dost thou come

To start my quiet.

RODERIGO.

Sir, sir, sir,—

BRABANTIO.

But thou must needs be sure

My spirit and my place have in them power

To make this bitter to thee.

RODERIGO.

Patience, good sir.

BRABANTIO.

What tell'st thou me of robbing?

This is Venice. My house is not a grange.

RODERIGO.

Most grave Brabantio,

In simple and pure soul I come to you.

IAGO.

Zounds, sir, you are one of those that will not serve God if the devil bid you. Because we come to do you service, and you think we are ruffians, you'll have your daughter cover'd with a Barbary horse; you'll have your nephews neigh to you; you'll have coursers for cousins and gennets for germans.

BRABANTIO.

What profane wretch art thou?

IAGO.

I am one, sir, that comes to tell you your daughter and the Moor are now making the beast with two backs.

BRABANTIO.

Thou art a villain.

IAGO.

You are a senator.

BRABANTIO.

This thou shalt answer. I know thee, Roderigo.

RODERIGO.

Sir, I will answer anything. But I beseech you,

If 't be your pleasure, and most wise consent,

(As partly I find it is) that your fair daughter,

At this odd-even and dull watch o' the night,

Transported with no worse nor better guard,

But with a knave of common hire, a gondolier,

To the gross clasps of a lascivious Moor:

If this be known to you, and your allowance,

We then have done you bold and saucy wrongs.

But if you know not this, my manners tell me,

We have your wrong rebuke. Do not believe

That from the sense of all civility,

I thus would play and trifle with your reverence.

Your daughter (if you have not given her leave)

I say again, hath made a gross revolt,

Tying her duty, beauty, wit, and fortunes

In an extravagant and wheeling stranger

Of here and everywhere. Straight satisfy yourself:

If she be in her chamber or your house,

Let loose on me the justice of the state

For thus deluding you.

BRABANTIO.

Strike on the tinder, ho!

Give me a taper! Call up all my people!

This accident is not unlike my dream,

Belief of it oppresses me already.

Light, I say, light!

[Exit from above.]

IAGO.

Farewell; for I must leave you:

It seems not meet nor wholesome to my place

To be produc'd, as if I stay I shall,

Against the Moor. For I do know the state,

However this may gall him with some check,

Cannot with safety cast him, for he's embark'd

With such loud reason to the Cyprus wars,

Which even now stand in act, that, for their souls,

Another of his fathom they have none

To lead their business. In which regard,

Though I do hate him as I do hell pains,

Yet, for necessity of present life,

I must show out a flag and sign of love,

Which is indeed but sign. That you shall surely find him,

Lead to the Sagittary the raised search,

And there will I be with him. So, farewell.

[Exit.]

Enter Brabantio with Servants and torches.

BRABANTIO.

It is too true an evil. Gone she is,

And what's to come of my despised time,

Is naught but bitterness. Now Roderigo,

Where didst thou see her? (O unhappy girl!)

With the Moor, say'st thou? (Who would be a father!)

How didst thou know 'twas she? (O, she deceives me

Past thought.) What said she to you? Get more tapers,

Raise all my kindred. Are they married, think you?

RODERIGO.

Truly I think they are.

BRABANTIO.

O heaven! How got she out? O treason of the blood!

Fathers, from hence trust not your daughters' minds

By what you see them act. Is there not charms

By which the property of youth and maidhood

May be abused? Have you not read, Roderigo,

Of some such thing?

RODERIGO.

Yes, sir, I have indeed.

BRABANTIO.

Call up my brother. O, would you had had her!

Some one way, some another. Do you know

Where we may apprehend her and the Moor?

RODERIGO.

I think I can discover him, if you please

To get good guard, and go along with me.

BRABANTIO.

Pray you lead on. At every house I'll call,

I may command at most. Get weapons, ho!

And raise some special officers of night.

On, good Roderigo. I will deserve your pains.

[Exeunt.]

SCENE II. Venice. Another street.

Enter Othello, Iago and Attendants with torches.

IAGO.

Though in the trade of war I have slain men,

Yet do I hold it very stuff o' the conscience

To do no contriv'd murder; I lack iniquity

Sometimes to do me service: nine or ten times

I had thought to have yerk'd him here under the ribs.

OTHELLO.

'Tis better as it is.

IAGO.

Nay, but he prated,

And spoke such scurvy and provoking terms

Against your honour,

That with the little godliness I have,

I did full hard forbear him. But I pray you, sir,

Are you fast married? Be assur'd of this,

That the magnifico is much belov'd

And hath in his effect a voice potential

As double as the duke's; he will divorce you,

Or put upon you what restraint and grievance

The law (with all his might to enforce it on)

Will give him cable.

OTHELLO.

Let him do his spite;

My services, which I have done the signiory,

Shall out-tongue his complaints. 'Tis yet to know,—

Which, when I know that boasting is an honour,

I shall promulgate,—I fetch my life and being

From men of royal siege. And my demerits

May speak unbonneted to as proud a fortune

As this that I have reach'd. For know, Iago,

But that I love the gentle Desdemona,

I would not my unhoused free condition

Put into circumscription and confine

For the sea's worth. But look, what lights come yond?

IAGO.

Those are the raised father and his friends:

You were best go in.

OTHELLO.

Not I; I must be found.

My parts, my title, and my perfect soul

Shall manifest me rightly. Is it they?

IAGO.

By Janus, I think no.

Enter Cassio and Officers with torches.

OTHELLO.

The servants of the duke and my lieutenant.

The goodness of the night upon you, friends!

What is the news?

CASSIO.

The duke does greet you, general,

And he requires your haste-post-haste appearance

Even on the instant.

OTHELLO.

What is the matter, think you?

CASSIO.

Something from Cyprus, as I may divine.

It is a business of some heat. The galleys

Have sent a dozen sequent messengers

This very night at one another's heels;

And many of the consuls, rais'd and met,

Are at the duke's already. You have been hotly call'd for,

When, being not at your lodging to be found,

The senate hath sent about three several quests

To search you out.

OTHELLO.

'Tis well I am found by you.

I will but spend a word here in the house,

And go with you.

[Exit.]

CASSIO.

Ancient, what makes he here?

IAGO.

Faith, he tonight hath boarded a land carrack:

If it prove lawful prize, he's made forever.

CASSIO.

I do not understand.

IAGO.

He's married.

CASSIO.

To who?

Enter Othello.

IAGO.

Marry to—Come, captain, will you go?

OTHELLO.

Have with you.

CASSIO.

Here comes another troop to seek for you.

Enter Brabantio, Roderigo and Officers with torches and weapons.

IAGO.

It is Brabantio. General, be advis'd,

He comes to bad intent.

OTHELLO.

Holla, stand there!

RODERIGO.

Signior, it is the Moor.

BRABANTIO.

Down with him, thief!

[They draw on both sides.]

IAGO.

You, Roderigo! Come, sir, I am for you.

OTHELLO.

Keep up your bright swords, for the dew will rust them.

Good signior, you shall more command with years

Than with your weapons.

BRABANTIO.

O thou foul thief, where hast thou stow'd my daughter?

Damn'd as thou art, thou hast enchanted her,

For I'll refer me to all things of sense,

(If she in chains of magic were not bound)

Whether a maid so tender, fair, and happy,

So opposite to marriage, that she shunn'd

The wealthy curled darlings of our nation,

Would ever have, to incur a general mock,

Run from her guardage to the sooty bosom

Of such a thing as thou—to fear, not to delight.

Judge me the world, if 'tis not gross in sense,

That thou hast practis'd on her with foul charms,

Abus'd her delicate youth with drugs or minerals

That weakens motion. I'll have't disputed on;

'Tis probable, and palpable to thinking.

I therefore apprehend and do attach thee

For an abuser of the world, a practiser

Of arts inhibited and out of warrant.—

Lay hold upon him, if he do resist,

Subdue him at his peril.

OTHELLO.

Hold your hands,

Both you of my inclining and the rest:

Were it my cue to fight, I should have known it

Without a prompter. Where will you that I go

To answer this your charge?

BRABANTIO.

To prison, till fit time

Of law and course of direct session

Call thee to answer.

OTHELLO.

What if I do obey?

How may the duke be therewith satisfied,

Whose messengers are here about my side,

Upon some present business of the state,

To bring me to him?

OFFICER.

'Tis true, most worthy signior,

The duke's in council, and your noble self,

I am sure is sent for.

BRABANTIO.

How? The duke in council?

In this time of the night? Bring him away;

Mine's not an idle cause. The duke himself,

Or any of my brothers of the state,

Cannot but feel this wrong as 'twere their own.

For if such actions may have passage free,

Bond-slaves and pagans shall our statesmen be.

[Exeunt.]

SCENE III. Venice. A council chamber.

The Duke and Senators sitting at a table; Officers attending.

DUKE.

There is no composition in these news

That gives them credit.

FIRST SENATOR.

Indeed, they are disproportion'd;

My letters say a hundred and seven galleys.

DUKE.

And mine a hundred and forty.

SECOND SENATOR

And mine two hundred:

But though they jump not on a just account,

(As in these cases, where the aim reports,

'Tis oft with difference,) yet do they all confirm

A Turkish fleet, and bearing up to Cyprus.

DUKE.

Nay, it is possible enough to judgement:

I do not so secure me in the error,

But the main article I do approve

In fearful sense.

SAILOR.

[Within.] What, ho! what, ho! what, ho!

OFFICER.

A messenger from the galleys.

Enter Sailor.

DUKE.

Now,—what's the business?

SAILOR.

The Turkish preparation makes for Rhodes,

So was I bid report here to the state

By Signior Angelo.

DUKE.

How say you by this change?

FIRST SENATOR.

This cannot be

By no assay of reason. 'Tis a pageant

To keep us in false gaze. When we consider

The importancy of Cyprus to the Turk;

And let ourselves again but understand

That, as it more concerns the Turk than Rhodes,

So may he with more facile question bear it,

For that it stands not in such warlike brace,

But altogether lacks the abilities

That Rhodes is dress'd in. If we make thought of this,

We must not think the Turk is so unskilful

To leave that latest which concerns him first,

Neglecting an attempt of ease and gain,

To wake and wage a danger profitless.

DUKE.

Nay, in all confidence, he's not for Rhodes.

OFFICER.

Here is more news.

Enter a Messenger.

MESSENGER.

The Ottomites, reverend and gracious,

Steering with due course toward the isle of Rhodes,

Have there injointed them with an after fleet.

FIRST SENATOR.

Ay, so I thought. How many, as you guess?

MESSENGER.

Of thirty sail, and now they do re-stem

Their backward course, bearing with frank appearance

Their purposes toward Cyprus. Signior Montano,

Your trusty and most valiant servitor,

With his free duty recommends you thus,

And prays you to believe him.

DUKE.

'Tis certain, then, for Cyprus.

Marcus Luccicos, is not he in town?

FIRST SENATOR.

He's now in Florence.

DUKE.

Write from us to him; post-post-haste dispatch.

FIRST SENATOR.

Here comes Brabantio and the valiant Moor.

Enter Brabantio, Othello, Iago, Roderigo and Officers.

DUKE.

Valiant Othello, we must straight employ you

Against the general enemy Ottoman.

[To Brabantio.] I did not see you; welcome, gentle signior,

We lack'd your counsel and your help tonight.

BRABANTIO.

So did I yours. Good your grace, pardon me.

Neither my place, nor aught I heard of business

Hath rais'd me from my bed, nor doth the general care

Take hold on me; for my particular grief

Is of so flood-gate and o'erbearing nature

That it engluts and swallows other sorrows,

And it is still itself.

DUKE.

Why, what's the matter?

BRABANTIO.

My daughter! O, my daughter!

DUKE and SENATORS.

Dead?

BRABANTIO.

Ay, to me.

She is abused, stol'n from me, and corrupted

By spells and medicines bought of mountebanks;

For nature so preposterously to err,

Being not deficient, blind, or lame of sense,

Sans witchcraft could not.

DUKE.

Whoe'er he be, that in this foul proceeding,

Hath thus beguil'd your daughter of herself,

And you of her, the bloody book of law

You shall yourself read in the bitter letter,

After your own sense, yea, though our proper son

Stood in your action.

BRABANTIO.

Humbly I thank your grace.

Here is the man, this Moor, whom now it seems

Your special mandate for the state affairs

Hath hither brought.

ALL.

We are very sorry for 't.

DUKE.

[To Othello.] What, in your own part, can you say to this?

BRABANTIO.

Nothing, but this is so.

OTHELLO.

Most potent, grave, and reverend signiors,

My very noble and approv'd good masters:

That I have ta'en away this old man's daughter,

It is most true; true, I have married her.

The very head and front of my offending

Hath this extent, no more. Rude am I in my speech,

And little bless'd with the soft phrase of peace;

For since these arms of mine had seven years' pith,

Till now some nine moons wasted, they have us'd

Their dearest action in the tented field,

And little of this great world can I speak,

More than pertains to feats of broil and battle,

And therefore little shall I grace my cause

In speaking for myself. Yet, by your gracious patience,

I will a round unvarnish'd tale deliver

Of my whole course of love: what drugs, what charms,

What conjuration, and what mighty magic,

(For such proceeding I am charged withal)

I won his daughter.

BRABANTIO.

A maiden never bold:

Of spirit so still and quiet that her motion

Blush'd at herself; and she, in spite of nature,

Of years, of country, credit, everything,

To fall in love with what she fear'd to look on!

It is judgement maim'd and most imperfect

That will confess perfection so could err

Against all rules of nature, and must be driven

To find out practices of cunning hell,

Why this should be. I therefore vouch again,

That with some mixtures powerful o'er the blood,

Or with some dram conjur'd to this effect,

He wrought upon her.

DUKE.

To vouch this is no proof;

Without more wider and more overt test

Than these thin habits and poor likelihoods

Of modern seeming do prefer against him.

FIRST SENATOR.

But, Othello, speak:

Did you by indirect and forced courses

Subdue and poison this young maid's affections?

Or came it by request, and such fair question

As soul to soul affordeth?

OTHELLO.

I do beseech you,

Send for the lady to the Sagittary,

And let her speak of me before her father.

If you do find me foul in her report,

The trust, the office I do hold of you,

Not only take away, but let your sentence

Even fall upon my life.

DUKE.

Fetch Desdemona hither.

OTHELLO.

Ancient, conduct them, you best know the place.

[Exeunt Iago and Attendants.]

And till she come, as truly as to heaven

I do confess the vices of my blood,

So justly to your grave ears I'll present

How I did thrive in this fair lady's love,

And she in mine.

DUKE.

Say it, Othello.

OTHELLO.

Her father lov'd me, oft invited me,

Still question'd me the story of my life,

From year to year—the battles, sieges, fortunes,

That I have pass'd.

I ran it through, even from my boyish days

To the very moment that he bade me tell it,

Wherein I spake of most disastrous chances,

Of moving accidents by flood and field;

Of hair-breadth scapes i' th' imminent deadly breach;

Of being taken by the insolent foe,

And sold to slavery, of my redemption thence,

And portance in my traveler's history,

Wherein of antres vast and deserts idle,

Rough quarries, rocks, and hills whose heads touch heaven,

It was my hint to speak,—such was the process;

And of the Cannibals that each other eat,

The Anthropophagi, and men whose heads

Do grow beneath their shoulders. This to hear

Would Desdemona seriously incline.

But still the house affairs would draw her thence,

Which ever as she could with haste dispatch,

She'd come again, and with a greedy ear

Devour up my discourse; which I observing,

Took once a pliant hour, and found good means

To draw from her a prayer of earnest heart

That I would all my pilgrimage dilate,

Whereof by parcels she had something heard,

But not intentively. I did consent,

And often did beguile her of her tears,

When I did speak of some distressful stroke

That my youth suffer'd. My story being done,

She gave me for my pains a world of sighs.

She swore, in faith, 'twas strange, 'twas passing strange;

'Twas pitiful, 'twas wondrous pitiful.

She wish'd she had not heard it, yet she wish'd

That heaven had made her such a man: she thank'd me,

And bade me, if I had a friend that lov'd her,

I should but teach him how to tell my story,

And that would woo her. Upon this hint I spake:

She lov'd me for the dangers I had pass'd,

And I lov'd her that she did pity them.

This only is the witchcraft I have us'd.

Here comes the lady. Let her witness it.

Enter Desdemona, Iago and Attendants.

DUKE.

I think this tale would win my daughter too.

Good Brabantio,

Take up this mangled matter at the best.

Men do their broken weapons rather use

Than their bare hands.

BRABANTIO.

I pray you hear her speak.

If she confess that she was half the wooer,

Destruction on my head, if my bad blame

Light on the man!—Come hither, gentle mistress:

Do you perceive in all this noble company

Where most you owe obedience?

DESDEMONA.

My noble father,

I do perceive here a divided duty:

To you I am bound for life and education.

My life and education both do learn me

How to respect you. You are the lord of duty,

I am hitherto your daughter: but here's my husband.

And so much duty as my mother show'd

To you, preferring you before her father,

So much I challenge that I may profess

Due to the Moor my lord.

BRABANTIO.

God be with you! I have done.

Please it your grace, on to the state affairs.

I had rather to adopt a child than get it.—

Come hither, Moor:

I here do give thee that with all my heart

Which, but thou hast already, with all my heart

I would keep from thee.—For your sake, jewel,

I am glad at soul I have no other child,

For thy escape would teach me tyranny,

To hang clogs on them.—I have done, my lord.

DUKE.

Let me speak like yourself, and lay a sentence,

Which as a grise or step may help these lovers

Into your favour.

When remedies are past, the griefs are ended

By seeing the worst, which late on hopes depended.

To mourn a mischief that is past and gone

Is the next way to draw new mischief on.

What cannot be preserved when fortune takes,

Patience her injury a mockery makes.

The robb'd that smiles steals something from the thief;

He robs himself that spends a bootless grief.

BRABANTIO.

So let the Turk of Cyprus us beguile,

We lose it not so long as we can smile;

He bears the sentence well, that nothing bears

But the free comfort which from thence he hears;

But he bears both the sentence and the sorrow

That, to pay grief, must of poor patience borrow.

These sentences to sugar or to gall,

Being strong on both sides, are equivocal:

But words are words; I never yet did hear

That the bruis'd heart was pierced through the ear.

I humbly beseech you, proceed to the affairs of state.

DUKE.

The Turk with a most mighty preparation makes for Cyprus. Othello, the fortitude of the place is best known to you. And though we have there a substitute of most allowed sufficiency, yet opinion, a sovereign mistress of effects, throws a more safer voice on you: you must therefore be content to slubber the gloss of your new fortunes with this more stubborn and boisterous expedition.

OTHELLO.

The tyrant custom, most grave senators,

Hath made the flinty and steel couch of war

My thrice-driven bed of down: I do agnize

A natural and prompt alacrity

I find in hardness, and do undertake

This present wars against the Ottomites.

Most humbly, therefore, bending to your state,

I crave fit disposition for my wife,

Due reference of place and exhibition,

With such accommodation and besort

As levels with her breeding.

DUKE.

If you please,

Be't at her father's.

BRABANTIO.

I'll not have it so.

OTHELLO.

Nor I.

DESDEMONA.

Nor I. I would not there reside,

To put my father in impatient thoughts,

By being in his eye. Most gracious duke,

To my unfolding lend your prosperous ear,

And let me find a charter in your voice

T' assist my simpleness.

DUKE.

What would you, Desdemona?

DESDEMONA.

That I did love the Moor to live with him,

My downright violence and storm of fortunes

May trumpet to the world: my heart's subdued

Even to the very quality of my lord.

I saw Othello's visage in his mind,

And to his honours and his valiant parts

Did I my soul and fortunes consecrate.

So that, dear lords, if I be left behind,

A moth of peace, and he go to the war,

The rites for which I love him are bereft me,

And I a heavy interim shall support

By his dear absence. Let me go with him.

OTHELLO.

Let her have your voice.

Vouch with me, heaven, I therefore beg it not

To please the palate of my appetite,

Nor to comply with heat, the young affects

In me defunct, and proper satisfaction,

But to be free and bounteous to her mind.

And heaven defend your good souls that you think

I will your serious and great business scant

For she is with me. No, when light-wing'd toys

Of feather'd Cupid seel with wanton dullness

My speculative and offic'd instruments,

That my disports corrupt and taint my business,

Let housewives make a skillet of my helm,

And all indign and base adversities

Make head against my estimation.

DUKE.

Be it as you shall privately determine,

Either for her stay or going. The affair cries haste,

And speed must answer it.

FIRST SENATOR.

You must away tonight.

OTHELLO.

With all my heart.

DUKE.

At nine i' the morning here we'll meet again.

Othello, leave some officer behind,

And he shall our commission bring to you,

With such things else of quality and respect

As doth import you.

OTHELLO.

So please your grace, my ancient,

A man he is of honesty and trust,

To his conveyance I assign my wife,

With what else needful your good grace shall think

To be sent after me.

DUKE.

Let it be so.

Good night to everyone. [To Brabantio.] And, noble signior,

If virtue no delighted beauty lack,

Your son-in-law is far more fair than black.

FIRST SENATOR.

Adieu, brave Moor, use Desdemona well.

BRABANTIO.

Look to her, Moor, if thou hast eyes to see:

She has deceiv'd her father, and may thee.

[Exeunt Duke, Senators, Officers, &c.]

OTHELLO.

My life upon her faith! Honest Iago,

My Desdemona must I leave to thee.

I prithee, let thy wife attend on her,

And bring them after in the best advantage.—

Come, Desdemona, I have but an hour

Of love, of worldly matters, and direction,

To spend with thee. We must obey the time.

[Exeunt Othello and Desdemona.]

RODERIGO.

Iago—

IAGO.

What sayst thou, noble heart?

RODERIGO.

What will I do, thinkest thou?

IAGO.

Why, go to bed and sleep.

RODERIGO.

I will incontinently drown myself.

IAGO.

If thou dost, I shall never love thee after. Why, thou silly gentleman!

RODERIGO.

It is silliness to live, when to live is torment; and then have we a prescription to die when death is our physician.

IAGO.

O villainous! I have looked upon the world for four times seven years, and since I could distinguish betwixt a benefit and an injury, I never found man that knew how to love himself. Ere I would say I would drown myself for the love of a guinea-hen, I would change my humanity with a baboon.

RODERIGO.

What should I do? I confess it is my shame to be so fond, but it is not in my virtue to amend it.

IAGO.

Virtue! a fig! 'Tis in ourselves that we are thus or thus. Our bodies are gardens, to the which our wills are gardeners. So that if we will plant nettles or sow lettuce, set hyssop and weed up thyme, supply it with one gender of herbs or distract it with many, either to have it sterile with idleness or manured with industry, why, the power and corrigible authority of this lies in our wills. If the balance of our lives had not one scale of reason to poise another of sensuality, the blood and baseness of our natures would conduct us to most preposterous conclusions. But we have reason to cool our raging motions, our carnal stings, our unbitted lusts; whereof I take this, that you call love, to be a sect, or scion.

RODERIGO.

It cannot be.

IAGO.

It is merely a lust of the blood and a permission of the will. Come, be a man. Drown thyself? Drown cats and blind puppies. I have professed me thy friend, and I confess me knit to thy deserving with cables of perdurable toughness; I could never better stead thee than now. Put money in thy purse; follow thou the wars; defeat thy favour with an usurped beard; I say, put money in thy purse. It cannot be that Desdemona should long continue her love to the Moor,—put money in thy purse,—nor he his to her. It was a violent commencement, and thou shalt see an answerable sequestration—put but money in thy purse. These Moors are changeable in their wills. Fill thy purse with money. The food that to him now is as luscious as locusts shall be to him shortly as acerb as the coloquintida. She must change for youth. When she is sated with his body, she will find the error of her choice. She must have change, she must. Therefore put money in thy purse. If thou wilt needs damn thyself, do it a more delicate way than drowning. Make all the money thou canst. If sanctimony and a frail vow betwixt an erring barbarian and a supersubtle Venetian be not too hard for my wits and all the tribe of hell, thou shalt enjoy her; therefore make money. A pox of drowning thyself! It is clean out of the way: seek thou rather to be hanged in compassing thy joy than to be drowned and go without her.

RODERIGO.

Wilt thou be fast to my hopes if I depend on the issue?

IAGO.

Thou art sure of me. Go, make money. I have told thee often, and I retell thee again and again, I hate the Moor. My cause is hearted; thine hath no less reason. Let us be conjunctive in our revenge against him: if thou canst cuckold him, thou dost thyself a pleasure, me a sport. There are many events in the womb of time which will be delivered. Traverse, go, provide thy money. We will have more of this tomorrow. Adieu.

RODERIGO.

Where shall we meet i' the morning?

IAGO.

At my lodging.

RODERIGO.

I'll be with thee betimes.

IAGO.

Go to, farewell. Do you hear, Roderigo?

RODERIGO.

What say you?

IAGO.

No more of drowning, do you hear?

RODERIGO.

I am changed. I'll sell all my land.

[Exit.]

IAGO.

Thus do I ever make my fool my purse.

For I mine own gain'd knowledge should profane

If I would time expend with such a snipe

But for my sport and profit. I hate the Moor,

And it is thought abroad that 'twixt my sheets

He has done my office. I know not if 't be true,

But I, for mere suspicion in that kind,

Will do as if for surety. He holds me well,

The better shall my purpose work on him.

Cassio's a proper man. Let me see now,

To get his place, and to plume up my will

In double knavery. How, how? Let's see.

After some time, to abuse Othello's ear

That he is too familiar with his wife.

He hath a person and a smooth dispose,

To be suspected, fram'd to make women false.

The Moor is of a free and open nature

That thinks men honest that but seem to be so,

And will as tenderly be led by the nose

As asses are.

I have't. It is engender'd. Hell and night

Must bring this monstrous birth to the world's light.

[Exit.]

ACT II

SCENE I. A seaport in Cyprus. A Platform.

Enter Montano and two Gentlemen.

MONTANO.

What from the cape can you discern at sea?

FIRST GENTLEMAN.

Nothing at all, it is a high-wrought flood.

I cannot 'twixt the heaven and the main

Descry a sail.

MONTANO.

Methinks the wind hath spoke aloud at land.

A fuller blast ne'er shook our battlements.

If it hath ruffian'd so upon the sea,

What ribs of oak, when mountains melt on them,

Can hold the mortise? What shall we hear of this?

SECOND GENTLEMAN.

A segregation of the Turkish fleet.

For do but stand upon the foaming shore,

The chidden billow seems to pelt the clouds,

The wind-shak'd surge, with high and monstrous main,

Seems to cast water on the burning Bear,

And quench the guards of the ever-fixed pole;

I never did like molestation view

On the enchafed flood.

MONTANO.

If that the Turkish fleet

Be not enshelter'd, and embay'd, they are drown'd.

It is impossible to bear it out.

Enter a third Gentleman.

THIRD GENTLEMAN.

News, lads! Our wars are done.

The desperate tempest hath so bang'd the Turks

That their designment halts. A noble ship of Venice

Hath seen a grievous wreck and sufferance

On most part of their fleet.

MONTANO.

How? Is this true?

THIRD GENTLEMAN.

The ship is here put in,

A Veronessa; Michael Cassio,

Lieutenant to the warlike Moor Othello,

Is come on shore; the Moor himself at sea,

And is in full commission here for Cyprus.

MONTANO.

I am glad on't. 'Tis a worthy governor.

THIRD GENTLEMAN.

But this same Cassio, though he speak of comfort

Touching the Turkish loss, yet he looks sadly,

And prays the Moor be safe; for they were parted

With foul and violent tempest.

MONTANO.

Pray heavens he be;

For I have serv'd him, and the man commands

Like a full soldier. Let's to the sea-side, ho!

As well to see the vessel that's come in

As to throw out our eyes for brave Othello,

Even till we make the main and the aerial blue

An indistinct regard.

THIRD GENTLEMAN.

Come, let's do so;

For every minute is expectancy

Of more arrivance.

Enter Cassio.

CASSIO.

Thanks you, the valiant of this warlike isle,

That so approve the Moor! O, let the heavens

Give him defence against the elements,

For I have lost him on a dangerous sea.

MONTANO.

Is he well shipp'd?

CASSIO.

His bark is stoutly timber'd, and his pilot

Of very expert and approv'd allowance;

Therefore my hopes, not surfeited to death,

Stand in bold cure.

[Within.] A sail, a sail, a sail!

Enter a Messenger.

CASSIO.

What noise?

MESSENGER.

The town is empty; on the brow o' the sea

Stand ranks of people, and they cry "A sail!"

CASSIO.

My hopes do shape him for the governor.

[A shot.]

SECOND GENTLEMAN.

They do discharge their shot of courtesy.

Our friends at least.

CASSIO.

I pray you, sir, go forth,

And give us truth who 'tis that is arriv'd.

SECOND GENTLEMAN.

I shall.

[Exit.]

MONTANO.

But, good lieutenant, is your general wiv'd?

CASSIO.

Most fortunately: he hath achiev'd a maid

That paragons description and wild fame,

One that excels the quirks of blazoning pens,

And in the essential vesture of creation

Does tire the ingener.

Enter second Gentleman.

How now? Who has put in?

SECOND GENTLEMAN.

'Tis one Iago, ancient to the general.

CASSIO.

He has had most favourable and happy speed:

Tempests themselves, high seas, and howling winds,

The gutter'd rocks, and congregated sands,

Traitors ensteep'd to clog the guiltless keel,

As having sense of beauty, do omit

Their mortal natures, letting go safely by

The divine Desdemona.

MONTANO.

What is she?

CASSIO.

She that I spake of, our great captain's captain,

Left in the conduct of the bold Iago;

Whose footing here anticipates our thoughts

A se'nnight's speed. Great Jove, Othello guard,

And swell his sail with thine own powerful breath,

That he may bless this bay with his tall ship,

Make love's quick pants in Desdemona's arms,

Give renew'd fire to our extincted spirits,

And bring all Cyprus comfort!

Enter Desdemona, Iago, Roderigo, and Emilia.

O, behold,

The riches of the ship is come on shore!

Ye men of Cyprus, let her have your knees.

Hail to thee, lady! and the grace of heaven,

Before, behind thee, and on every hand,

Enwheel thee round!

DESDEMONA.

I thank you, valiant Cassio.

What tidings can you tell me of my lord?

CASSIO.

He is not yet arrived, nor know I aught

But that he's well, and will be shortly here.

DESDEMONA.

O, but I fear—How lost you company?

[Within.] A sail, a sail!

CASSIO.

The great contention of the sea and skies

Parted our fellowship. But, hark! a sail.

[Guns within.]

SECOND GENTLEMAN.

They give their greeting to the citadel.

This likewise is a friend.

CASSIO.

See for the news.

[Exit Gentleman.]

Good ancient, you are welcome. [To Emilia.] Welcome, mistress.

Let it not gall your patience, good Iago,

That I extend my manners; 'tis my breeding

That gives me this bold show of courtesy.

[Kissing her.]

IAGO.

Sir, would she give you so much of her lips

As of her tongue she oft bestows on me,

You would have enough.

DESDEMONA.

Alas, she has no speech.

IAGO.

In faith, too much.

I find it still when I have list to sleep.

Marry, before your ladyship, I grant,

She puts her tongue a little in her heart,

And chides with thinking.

EMILIA.

You have little cause to say so.

IAGO.

Come on, come on; you are pictures out of doors,

Bells in your parlours, wild-cats in your kitchens,

Saints in your injuries, devils being offended,

Players in your housewifery, and housewives in your beds.

DESDEMONA.

O, fie upon thee, slanderer!

IAGO.

Nay, it is true, or else I am a Turk.

You rise to play, and go to bed to work.

EMILIA.

You shall not write my praise.

IAGO.

No, let me not.

DESDEMONA.

What wouldst thou write of me, if thou shouldst praise me?

IAGO.

O gentle lady, do not put me to't,

For I am nothing if not critical.

DESDEMONA.

Come on, assay.—There's one gone to the harbour?

IAGO.

Ay, madam.

DESDEMONA.

I am not merry, but I do beguile

The thing I am, by seeming otherwise.—

Come, how wouldst thou praise me?

IAGO.

I am about it, but indeed, my invention

Comes from my pate as birdlime does from frieze,

It plucks out brains and all: but my Muse labours,

And thus she is deliver'd.

If she be fair and wise, fairness and wit,

The one's for use, the other useth it.

DESDEMONA.

Well prais'd! How if she be black and witty?

IAGO.

If she be black, and thereto have a wit,

She'll find a white that shall her blackness fit.

DESDEMONA.

Worse and worse.

EMILIA.

How if fair and foolish?

IAGO.

She never yet was foolish that was fair,

For even her folly help'd her to an heir.

DESDEMONA.

These are old fond paradoxes to make fools laugh i' the alehouse. What miserable praise hast thou for her that's foul and foolish?

IAGO.

There's none so foul and foolish thereunto,

But does foul pranks which fair and wise ones do.

DESDEMONA.

O heavy ignorance! Thou praisest the worst best. But what praise couldst thou bestow on a deserving woman indeed, one that in the authority of her merit did justly put on the vouch of very malice itself?

IAGO.

She that was ever fair and never proud,

Had tongue at will and yet was never loud,

Never lack'd gold and yet went never gay,

Fled from her wish, and yet said, "Now I may";

She that, being anger'd, her revenge being nigh,

Bade her wrong stay and her displeasure fly;

She that in wisdom never was so frail

To change the cod's head for the salmon's tail;

She that could think and ne'er disclose her mind,

See suitors following and not look behind;

She was a wight, if ever such wight were—

DESDEMONA.

To do what?

IAGO.

To suckle fools and chronicle small beer.

DESDEMONA.

O most lame and impotent conclusion!—Do not learn of him, Emilia, though he be thy husband.—How say you, Cassio? is he not a most profane and liberal counsellor?

CASSIO.

He speaks home, madam. You may relish him more in the soldier than in the scholar.

IAGO.

[Aside.] He takes her by the palm. Ay, well said, whisper. With as little a web as this will I ensnare as great a fly as Cassio. Ay, smile upon her, do. I will gyve thee in thine own courtship. You say true, 'tis so, indeed. If such tricks as these strip you out of your lieutenantry, it had been better you had not kissed your three fingers so oft, which now again you are most apt to play the sir in. Very good; well kissed, an excellent courtesy! 'Tis so, indeed. Yet again your fingers to your lips? Would they were clyster-pipes for your sake!

[Trumpets within.]

The Moor! I know his trumpet.

CASSIO.

'Tis truly so.

DESDEMONA.

Let's meet him, and receive him.

CASSIO.

Lo, where he comes!

Enter Othello and Attendants.

OTHELLO.

O my fair warrior!

DESDEMONA.

My dear Othello!

OTHELLO.

It gives me wonder great as my content

To see you here before me. O my soul's joy!

If after every tempest come such calms,

May the winds blow till they have waken'd death!

And let the labouring bark climb hills of seas

Olympus-high, and duck again as low

As hell's from heaven! If it were now to die,

'Twere now to be most happy, for I fear

My soul hath her content so absolute

That not another comfort like to this

Succeeds in unknown fate.

DESDEMONA.

The heavens forbid

But that our loves and comforts should increase

Even as our days do grow!

OTHELLO.

Amen to that, sweet powers!

I cannot speak enough of this content.

It stops me here; it is too much of joy:

And this, and this, the greatest discords be [They kiss.]

That e'er our hearts shall make!

IAGO.

[Aside.] O, you are well tun'd now,

But I'll set down the pegs that make this music,

As honest as I am.

OTHELLO.

Come, let us to the castle.—

News, friends, our wars are done, the Turks are drown'd.

How does my old acquaintance of this isle?

Honey, you shall be well desir'd in Cyprus;

I have found great love amongst them. O my sweet,

I prattle out of fashion, and I dote

In mine own comforts.—I prithee, good Iago,

Go to the bay and disembark my coffers.

Bring thou the master to the citadel;

He is a good one, and his worthiness

Does challenge much respect.—Come, Desdemona,

Once more well met at Cyprus.

[Exeunt Othello, Desdemona and Attendants.]

IAGO.

Do thou meet me presently at the harbour. Come hither. If thou be'st valiant—as, they say, base men being in love have then a nobility in their natures more than is native to them—list me. The lieutenant tonight watches on the court of guard: first, I must tell thee this: Desdemona is directly in love with him.

RODERIGO.

With him? Why, 'tis not possible.

IAGO.

Lay thy finger thus, and let thy soul be instructed. Mark me with what violence she first loved the Moor, but for bragging, and telling her fantastical lies. And will she love him still for prating? Let not thy discreet heart think it. Her eye must be fed. And what delight shall she have to look on the devil? When the blood is made dull with the act of sport, there should be, again to inflame it and to give satiety a fresh appetite, loveliness in favour, sympathy in years, manners, and beauties; all which the Moor is defective in: now, for want of these required conveniences, her delicate tenderness will find itself abused, begin to heave the gorge, disrelish and abhor the Moor, very nature will instruct her in it, and compel her to some second choice. Now sir, this granted (as it is a most pregnant and unforced position) who stands so eminently in the degree of this fortune as Cassio does? a knave very voluble; no further conscionable than in putting on the mere form of civil and humane seeming, for the better compassing of his salt and most hidden loose affection? Why, none, why, none! A slipper and subtle knave, a finder out of occasions; that has an eye can stamp and counterfeit advantages, though true advantage never present itself: a devilish knave! Besides, the knave is handsome, young, and hath all those requisites in him that folly and green minds look after. A pestilent complete knave, and the woman hath found him already.

RODERIGO.

I cannot believe that in her, she is full of most blessed condition.

IAGO.

Blest fig's end! the wine she drinks is made of grapes: if she had been blessed, she would never have loved the Moor. Blessed pudding! Didst thou not see her paddle with the palm of his hand? Didst not mark that?

RODERIGO.

Yes, that I did. But that was but courtesy.

IAGO.

Lechery, by this hand. An index and obscure prologue to the history of lust and foul thoughts. They met so near with their lips that their breaths embrac'd together. Villainous thoughts, Roderigo! When these mutualities so marshal the way, hard at hand comes the master and main exercise, the incorporate conclusion. Pish! But, sir, be you ruled by me. I have brought you from Venice. Watch you tonight. For the command, I'll lay't upon you. Cassio knows you not. I'll not be far from you. Do you find some occasion to anger Cassio, either by speaking too loud, or tainting his discipline, or from what other course you please, which the time shall more favourably minister.

RODERIGO.

Well.

IAGO.

Sir, he is rash, and very sudden in choler, and haply with his truncheon may strike at you: provoke him that he may, for even out of that will I cause these of Cyprus to mutiny, whose qualification shall come into no true taste again but by the displanting of Cassio. So shall you have a shorter journey to your desires by the means I shall then have to prefer them, and the impediment most profitably removed, without the which there were no expectation of our prosperity.

RODERIGO.

I will do this, if I can bring it to any opportunity.

IAGO.

I warrant thee. Meet me by and by at the citadel: I must fetch his necessaries ashore. Farewell.

RODERIGO.

Adieu.

[Exit.]

IAGO.

That Cassio loves her, I do well believe it;

That she loves him, 'tis apt, and of great credit:

The Moor, howbeit that I endure him not,

Is of a constant, loving, noble nature;

And, I dare think, he'll prove to Desdemona

A most dear husband. Now, I do love her too,

Not out of absolute lust (though peradventure

I stand accountant for as great a sin)

But partly led to diet my revenge,

For that I do suspect the lusty Moor

Hath leap'd into my seat. The thought whereof

Doth, like a poisonous mineral, gnaw my inwards,

And nothing can or shall content my soul

Till I am even'd with him, wife for wife,

Or, failing so, yet that I put the Moor

At least into a jealousy so strong

That judgement cannot cure. Which thing to do,

If this poor trash of Venice, whom I trash

For his quick hunting, stand the putting on,

I'll have our Michael Cassio on the hip,

Abuse him to the Moor in the rank garb

(For I fear Cassio with my night-cap too)

Make the Moor thank me, love me, and reward me

For making him egregiously an ass

And practicing upon his peace and quiet

Even to madness. 'Tis here, but yet confus'd.

Knavery's plain face is never seen till us'd.

[Exit.]

SCENE II. A street.

Enter Othello's Herald with a proclamation.

HERALD.

It is Othello's pleasure, our noble and valiant general, that upon certain tidings now arrived, importing the mere perdition of the Turkish fleet, every man put himself into triumph: some to dance, some to make bonfires, each man to what sport and revels his addition leads him. For besides these beneficial news, it is the celebration of his nuptial. So much was his pleasure should be proclaimed. All offices are open, and there is full liberty of feasting from this present hour of five till the bell have told eleven. Heaven bless the isle of Cyprus and our noble general Othello!

[Exit.]

SCENE III. A Hall in the Castle.

Enter Othello, Desdemona, Cassio and Attendants.

OTHELLO.

Good Michael, look you to the guard tonight.

Let's teach ourselves that honourable stop,

Not to outsport discretion.

CASSIO.

Iago hath direction what to do.

But notwithstanding with my personal eye

Will I look to't.

OTHELLO.

Iago is most honest.

Michael, good night. Tomorrow with your earliest

Let me have speech with you. [To Desdemona.] Come, my dear love,

The purchase made, the fruits are to ensue;

That profit's yet to come 'tween me and you.—

Good night.

> [Exeunt Othello, Desdemona and Attendants.]
> **Enter Iago.**

CASSIO.

Welcome, Iago. We must to the watch.

IAGO.

Not this hour, lieutenant. 'Tis not yet ten o' th' clock. Our general cast us thus early for the love of his Desdemona; who let us not therefore blame: he hath not yet made wanton the night with her; and she is sport for Jove.

CASSIO.

She's a most exquisite lady.

IAGO.

And, I'll warrant her, full of game.

CASSIO.

Indeed, she is a most fresh and delicate creature.

IAGO.

What an eye she has! methinks it sounds a parley to provocation.

CASSIO.

An inviting eye, and yet methinks right modest.

IAGO.

And when she speaks, is it not an alarm to love?

CASSIO.

She is indeed perfection.

IAGO.

Well, happiness to their sheets! Come, lieutenant, I have a stoup of wine; and here without are a brace of Cyprus gallants that would fain have a measure to the health of black Othello.

CASSIO.

Not tonight, good Iago. I have very poor and unhappy brains for drinking. I could well wish courtesy would invent some other custom of entertainment.

IAGO.

O, they are our friends; but one cup: I'll drink for you.

CASSIO.

I have drunk but one cup tonight, and that was craftily qualified too, and behold, what innovation it makes here: I am unfortunate in the infirmity, and dare not task my weakness with any more.

IAGO.

What, man! 'Tis a night of revels. The gallants desire it.

CASSIO.

Where are they?

IAGO.

Here at the door. I pray you, call them in.

CASSIO.

I'll do't; but it dislikes me.

[Exit.]

IAGO.

If I can fasten but one cup upon him,

With that which he hath drunk tonight already,

He'll be as full of quarrel and offence

As my young mistress' dog. Now my sick fool Roderigo,

Whom love hath turn'd almost the wrong side out,

To Desdemona hath tonight carous'd

Potations pottle-deep; and he's to watch:

Three lads of Cyprus, noble swelling spirits,

That hold their honours in a wary distance,

The very elements of this warlike isle,

Have I tonight fluster'd with flowing cups,

And they watch too. Now, 'mongst this flock of drunkards,

Am I to put our Cassio in some action

That may offend the isle. But here they come:

If consequence do but approve my dream,

My boat sails freely, both with wind and stream.

Enter Cassio, Montano and Gentlemen; followed by Servant with wine.

CASSIO.

'Fore God, they have given me a rouse already.

MONTANO.

Good faith, a little one; not past a pint, as I am a soldier.

IAGO.

Some wine, ho!

[Sings.]

And let me the cannikin clink, clink,

And let me the cannikin clink, clink:

A soldier's a man,

O, man's life's but a span,

Why then let a soldier drink.

Some wine, boys!

CASSIO.

'Fore God, an excellent song.

71

IAGO.

I learned it in England, where indeed they are most potent in potting: your Dane, your German, and your swag-bellied Hollander,—drink, ho!— are nothing to your English.

CASSIO.

Is your Englishman so expert in his drinking?

IAGO.

Why, he drinks you, with facility, your Dane dead drunk; he sweats not to overthrow your Almain; he gives your Hollander a vomit ere the next pottle can be filled.

CASSIO.

To the health of our general!

MONTANO.

I am for it, lieutenant; and I'll do you justice.

IAGO.

O sweet England!

[Sings.]

King Stephen was a worthy peer,

  His breeches cost him but a crown;

He held them sixpence all too dear,

  With that he call'd the tailor lown.

He was a wight of high renown,

  And thou art but of low degree:

'Tis pride that pulls the country down,

  Then take thine auld cloak about thee.

Some wine, ho!

CASSIO.

'Fore God, this is a more exquisite song than the other.

IAGO.

Will you hear 't again?

CASSIO.

No, for I hold him to be unworthy of his place that does those things. Well, God's above all, and there be souls must be saved, and there be souls must not be saved.

IAGO.

It's true, good lieutenant.

CASSIO.

For mine own part, no offence to the general, nor any man of quality, I hope to be saved.

IAGO.

And so do I too, lieutenant.

CASSIO.

Ay, but, by your leave, not before me; the lieutenant is to be saved before the ancient. Let's have no more of this; let's to our affairs. Forgive us our sins! Gentlemen, let's look to our business. Do not think, gentlemen, I am drunk. This is my ancient, this is my right hand, and this is my left. I am not drunk now. I can stand well enough, and I speak well enough.

ALL.

Excellent well.

CASSIO.

Why, very well then. You must not think, then, that I am drunk.

[Exit.]

MONTANO.

To the platform, masters. Come, let's set the watch.

IAGO.

You see this fellow that is gone before,

He is a soldier fit to stand by Cæsar

And give direction: and do but see his vice,

'Tis to his virtue a just equinox,

The one as long as th' other. 'Tis pity of him.

I fear the trust Othello puts him in,

On some odd time of his infirmity,

Will shake this island.

MONTANO.

But is he often thus?

IAGO.

'Tis evermore the prologue to his sleep:

He'll watch the horologe a double set

If drink rock not his cradle.

MONTANO.

It were well

The general were put in mind of it.

Perhaps he sees it not, or his good nature

Prizes the virtue that appears in Cassio,

And looks not on his evils: is not this true?

Enter Roderigo.

IAGO.

[Aside to him.] How now, Roderigo?

I pray you, after the lieutenant; go.

[Exit Roderigo.]

MONTANO.

And 'tis great pity that the noble Moor

Should hazard such a place as his own second

With one of an ingraft infirmity:

It were an honest action to say so

To the Moor.

IAGO.

Not I, for this fair island.

I do love Cassio well and would do much

To cure him of this evil. But, hark! What noise?

[Cry within: "Help! help!"]

Enter Cassio, driving in Roderigo.

CASSIO.

Zounds, you rogue, you rascal!

MONTANO.

What's the matter, lieutenant?

CASSIO.

A knave teach me my duty! I'll beat the knave into a twiggen bottle.

RODERIGO.

Beat me?

CASSIO.

Dost thou prate, rogue?

[Striking Roderigo.]

MONTANO.

Nay, good lieutenant;

I pray you, sir, hold your hand.

CASSIO.

Let me go, sir,

Or I'll knock you o'er the mazard.

MONTANO.

Come, come, you're drunk.

CASSIO.

Drunk?

[They fight.]

IAGO.

[Aside to Roderigo.] Away, I say! Go out and cry a mutiny.

[Exit Roderigo.]

Nay, good lieutenant, God's will, gentlemen.

Help, ho!—Lieutenant,—sir,—Montano,—sir:—

Help, masters! Here's a goodly watch indeed!

[A bell rings.]

Who's that which rings the bell?—Diablo, ho!

The town will rise. God's will, lieutenant, hold,

You will be sham'd forever.

Enter Othello and Attendants.

OTHELLO.

What is the matter here?

MONTANO.

Zounds, I bleed still, I am hurt to the death.

OTHELLO.

Hold, for your lives!

IAGO.

Hold, ho! lieutenant,—sir,—Montano,—gentlemen,—

Have you forgot all place of sense and duty?

Hold! The general speaks to you; hold, hold, for shame!

OTHELLO.

Why, how now, ho! From whence ariseth this?

Are we turn'd Turks, and to ourselves do that

Which heaven hath forbid the Ottomites?

For Christian shame, put by this barbarous brawl:

He that stirs next to carve for his own rage

Holds his soul light; he dies upon his motion.

Silence that dreadful bell, it frights the isle

From her propriety. What is the matter, masters?

Honest Iago, that looks dead with grieving,

Speak, who began this? On thy love, I charge thee.

IAGO.

I do not know. Friends all but now, even now,

In quarter, and in terms like bride and groom

Devesting them for bed; and then, but now,

As if some planet had unwitted men,

Swords out, and tilting one at other's breast,

In opposition bloody. I cannot speak

Any beginning to this peevish odds;

And would in action glorious I had lost

Those legs that brought me to a part of it!

OTHELLO.

How comes it, Michael, you are thus forgot?

CASSIO.

I pray you, pardon me; I cannot speak.

OTHELLO.

Worthy Montano, you were wont be civil.

The gravity and stillness of your youth

The world hath noted, and your name is great

In mouths of wisest censure: what's the matter,

That you unlace your reputation thus,

And spend your rich opinion for the name

Of a night-brawler? Give me answer to it.

MONTANO.

Worthy Othello, I am hurt to danger.

Your officer, Iago, can inform you,

While I spare speech, which something now offends me,

Of all that I do know; nor know I aught

By me that's said or done amiss this night,

Unless self-charity be sometimes a vice,

And to defend ourselves it be a sin

When violence assails us.

OTHELLO.

Now, by heaven,

My blood begins my safer guides to rule,

And passion, having my best judgement collied,

Assays to lead the way. Zounds, if I stir,

Or do but lift this arm, the best of you

Shall sink in my rebuke. Give me to know

How this foul rout began, who set it on,

And he that is approv'd in this offence,

Though he had twinn'd with me, both at a birth,

Shall lose me. What! in a town of war,

Yet wild, the people's hearts brimful of fear,

To manage private and domestic quarrel,

In night, and on the court and guard of safety?

'Tis monstrous. Iago, who began't?

MONTANO.

If partially affin'd, or leagu'd in office,

Thou dost deliver more or less than truth,

Thou art no soldier.

IAGO.

Touch me not so near.

I had rather have this tongue cut from my mouth

Than it should do offence to Michael Cassio.

Yet I persuade myself, to speak the truth

Shall nothing wrong him. Thus it is, general:

Montano and myself being in speech,

There comes a fellow crying out for help,

And Cassio following him with determin'd sword,

To execute upon him. Sir, this gentleman

Steps in to Cassio and entreats his pause.

Myself the crying fellow did pursue,

Lest by his clamour (as it so fell out)

The town might fall in fright: he, swift of foot,

Outran my purpose: and I return'd the rather

For that I heard the clink and fall of swords,

And Cassio high in oath, which till tonight

I ne'er might say before. When I came back,

(For this was brief) I found them close together,

At blow and thrust, even as again they were

When you yourself did part them.

More of this matter cannot I report.

But men are men; the best sometimes forget;

Though Cassio did some little wrong to him,

As men in rage strike those that wish them best,

Yet surely Cassio, I believe, receiv'd

From him that fled some strange indignity,

Which patience could not pass.

OTHELLO.

I know, Iago,

Thy honesty and love doth mince this matter,

Making it light to Cassio. Cassio, I love thee,

But never more be officer of mine.

Enter Desdemona, attended.

Look, if my gentle love be not rais'd up!

I'll make thee an example.

DESDEMONA.

What's the matter?

OTHELLO.

All's well now, sweeting; come away to bed.

Sir, for your hurts, myself will be your surgeon.

Lead him off.

[Montano is led off.]

Iago, look with care about the town,

And silence those whom this vile brawl distracted.

Come, Desdemona: 'tis the soldiers' life

To have their balmy slumbers wak'd with strife.

[Exeunt all but Iago and Cassio.]

IAGO.

What, are you hurt, lieutenant?

CASSIO.

Ay, past all surgery.

IAGO.

Marry, Heaven forbid!

CASSIO.

Reputation, reputation, reputation! O, I have lost my reputation! I have lost the immortal part of myself, and what remains is bestial. My reputation, Iago, my reputation!

IAGO.

As I am an honest man, I thought you had received some bodily wound; there is more sense in that than in reputation. Reputation is an idle and most false imposition, oft got without merit and lost without deserving. You have lost no reputation at all, unless you repute yourself such a loser. What, man, there are ways to recover the general again: you are but now cast in his mood, a punishment more in policy than in malice, even so as one would beat his offenceless dog to affright an imperious lion: sue to him again, and he's yours.

CASSIO.

I will rather sue to be despised than to deceive so good a commander with so slight, so drunken, and so indiscreet an officer. Drunk? and speak parrot? and squabble? swagger? swear? and discourse fustian with one's own

82

shadow? O thou invisible spirit of wine, if thou hast no name to be known by, let us call thee devil!

IAGO.

What was he that you followed with your sword? What had he done to you?

CASSIO.

I know not.

IAGO.

Is't possible?

CASSIO.

I remember a mass of things, but nothing distinctly; a quarrel, but nothing wherefore. O God, that men should put an enemy in their mouths to steal away their brains! That we should with joy, pleasance, revel, and applause, transform ourselves into beasts!

IAGO.

Why, but you are now well enough: how came you thus recovered?

CASSIO.

It hath pleased the devil drunkenness to give place to the devil wrath. One unperfectness shows me another, to make me frankly despise myself.

IAGO.

Come, you are too severe a moraler. As the time, the place, and the condition of this country stands, I could heartily wish this had not befallen; but since it is as it is, mend it for your own good.

CASSIO.

I will ask him for my place again; he shall tell me I am a drunkard! Had I as many mouths as Hydra, such an answer would stop them all. To be now a sensible man, by and by a fool, and presently a beast! O strange! Every inordinate cup is unbless'd, and the ingredient is a devil.

IAGO.

Come, come, good wine is a good familiar creature, if it be well used. Exclaim no more against it. And, good lieutenant, I think you think I love you.

CASSIO.

I have well approved it, sir.—I drunk!

IAGO.

You, or any man living, may be drunk at a time, man. I'll tell you what you shall do. Our general's wife is now the general; I may say so in this respect, for that he hath devoted and given up himself to the contemplation, mark, and denotement of her parts and graces. Confess yourself freely to her. Importune her help to put you in your place again. She is of so free, so kind, so apt, so blessed a disposition, she holds it a vice in her goodness not to do more than she is requested. This broken joint between you and her husband entreat her to splinter, and, my fortunes against any lay worth naming, this crack of your love shall grow stronger than it was before.

CASSIO.

You advise me well.

IAGO.

I protest, in the sincerity of love and honest kindness.

CASSIO.

I think it freely; and betimes in the morning I will beseech the virtuous Desdemona to undertake for me; I am desperate of my fortunes if they check me here.

IAGO.

You are in the right. Good night, lieutenant, I must to the watch.

CASSIO.

Good night, honest Iago.

[Exit.]

IAGO.

And what's he then, that says I play the villain?

When this advice is free I give and honest,

Probal to thinking, and indeed the course

To win the Moor again? For 'tis most easy

The inclining Desdemona to subdue

In any honest suit. She's fram'd as fruitful

As the free elements. And then for her

To win the Moor, were't to renounce his baptism,

All seals and symbols of redeemed sin,

His soul is so enfetter'd to her love

That she may make, unmake, do what she list,

Even as her appetite shall play the god

With his weak function. How am I then, a villain

To counsel Cassio to this parallel course,

Directly to his good? Divinity of hell!

When devils will the blackest sins put on,

They do suggest at first with heavenly shows,

As I do now: for whiles this honest fool

Plies Desdemona to repair his fortune,

And she for him pleads strongly to the Moor,

I'll pour this pestilence into his ear,

That she repeals him for her body's lust;

And by how much she strives to do him good,

She shall undo her credit with the Moor.

So will I turn her virtue into pitch,

And out of her own goodness make the net

That shall enmesh them all.

Enter Roderigo.

How now, Roderigo?

RODERIGO.

I do follow here in the chase, not like a hound that hunts, but one that fills up the cry. My money is almost spent, I have been tonight exceedingly well cudgelled; and I think the issue will be, I shall have so much experience for my pains, and so, with no money at all and a little more wit, return again to Venice.

IAGO.

How poor are they that have not patience!

What wound did ever heal but by degrees?

Thou know'st we work by wit, and not by witchcraft,

And wit depends on dilatory time.

Does't not go well? Cassio hath beaten thee,

And thou, by that small hurt, hast cashier'd Cassio;

Though other things grow fair against the sun,

Yet fruits that blossom first will first be ripe.

Content thyself awhile. By the mass, 'tis morning;

Pleasure and action make the hours seem short.

Retire thee; go where thou art billeted.

Away, I say, thou shalt know more hereafter.

Nay, get thee gone.

[Exit Roderigo.]

Two things are to be done,

My wife must move for Cassio to her mistress.

I'll set her on;

Myself the while to draw the Moor apart,

And bring him jump when he may Cassio find

Soliciting his wife. Ay, that's the way.

Dull not device by coldness and delay.

[Exit.]

ACT III

SCENE I. Cyprus. Before the Castle.

Enter Cassio and some Musicians.

CASSIO.

Masters, play here, I will content your pains,

Something that's brief; and bid "Good morrow, general."

[Music.]

Enter Clown.

CLOWN.

Why, masters, have your instruments been in Naples, that they speak i' the nose thus?

FIRST MUSICIAN.

How, sir, how?

CLOWN.

Are these, I pray you, wind instruments?

FIRST MUSICIAN.

Ay, marry, are they, sir.

CLOWN.

O, thereby hangs a tail.

FIRST MUSICIAN.

Whereby hangs a tale, sir?

CLOWN.

Marry, sir, by many a wind instrument that I know. But, masters, here's money for you: and the general so likes your music, that he desires you, for love's sake, to make no more noise with it.

FIRST MUSICIAN.

Well, sir, we will not.

CLOWN.

If you have any music that may not be heard, to't again. But, as they say, to hear music the general does not greatly care.

FIRST MUSICIAN.

We have none such, sir.

CLOWN.

Then put up your pipes in your bag, for I'll away. Go, vanish into air, away!

[Exeunt Musicians.]

CASSIO.

Dost thou hear, mine honest friend?

CLOWN.

No, I hear not your honest friend. I hear you.

CASSIO.

Prithee, keep up thy quillets. There's a poor piece of gold for thee: if the gentlewoman that attends the general's wife be stirring, tell her there's one Cassio entreats her a little favour of speech. Wilt thou do this?

CLOWN.

She is stirring, sir; if she will stir hither, I shall seem to notify unto her.

CASSIO.

Do, good my friend.

[Exit Clown.]

Enter Iago.

In happy time, Iago.

IAGO.

You have not been a-bed, then?

CASSIO.

Why, no. The day had broke

Before we parted. I have made bold, Iago,

To send in to your wife. My suit to her

Is, that she will to virtuous Desdemona

Procure me some access.

IAGO.

I'll send her to you presently,

And I'll devise a mean to draw the Moor

Out of the way, that your converse and business

May be more free.

CASSIO.

I humbly thank you for't.

[Exit Iago.]

I never knew

A Florentine more kind and honest.

Enter Emilia.

EMILIA.

Good morrow, good lieutenant; I am sorry

For your displeasure, but all will sure be well.

The general and his wife are talking of it,

And she speaks for you stoutly: the Moor replies

That he you hurt is of great fame in Cyprus

And great affinity, and that in wholesome wisdom

He might not but refuse you; but he protests he loves you

And needs no other suitor but his likings

To take the safest occasion by the front

To bring you in again.

CASSIO.

Yet, I beseech you,

If you think fit, or that it may be done,

Give me advantage of some brief discourse

With Desdemona alone.

EMILIA.

Pray you, come in.

I will bestow you where you shall have time

To speak your bosom freely.

CASSIO.

I am much bound to you.

[Exeunt.]

SCENE II. Cyprus. A Room in the Castle.

Enter Othello, Iago and Gentlemen.

OTHELLO.

These letters give, Iago, to the pilot,

And by him do my duties to the senate.

That done, I will be walking on the works,

Repair there to me.

IAGO.

Well, my good lord, I'll do't.

OTHELLO.

This fortification, gentlemen, shall we see't?

GENTLEMEN.

We'll wait upon your lordship.

[Exeunt.]

SCENE III. Cyprus. The Garden of the Castle.

Enter Desdemona, Cassio and Emilia.

DESDEMONA.

Be thou assured, good Cassio, I will do

All my abilities in thy behalf.

EMILIA.

Good madam, do. I warrant it grieves my husband

As if the cause were his.

DESDEMONA.

O, that's an honest fellow. Do not doubt, Cassio,

But I will have my lord and you again

As friendly as you were.

CASSIO.

Bounteous madam,

Whatever shall become of Michael Cassio,

He's never anything but your true servant.

DESDEMONA.

I know't. I thank you. You do love my lord.

You have known him long; and be you well assur'd

He shall in strangeness stand no farther off

Than in a politic distance.

CASSIO.

Ay, but, lady,

That policy may either last so long,

Or feed upon such nice and waterish diet,

Or breed itself so out of circumstance,

That, I being absent, and my place supplied,

My general will forget my love and service.

DESDEMONA.

Do not doubt that. Before Emilia here

I give thee warrant of thy place. Assure thee,

If I do vow a friendship, I'll perform it

To the last article. My lord shall never rest,

I'll watch him tame, and talk him out of patience;

His bed shall seem a school, his board a shrift;

I'll intermingle everything he does

With Cassio's suit. Therefore be merry, Cassio,

For thy solicitor shall rather die

Than give thy cause away.

Enter Othello and Iago.

EMILIA.

Madam, here comes my lord.

CASSIO.

Madam, I'll take my leave.

DESDEMONA.

Why, stay, and hear me speak.

CASSIO.

Madam, not now. I am very ill at ease,

Unfit for mine own purposes.

DESDEMONA.

Well, do your discretion.

[Exit Cassio.]

IAGO.

Ha, I like not that.

OTHELLO.

What dost thou say?

IAGO.

Nothing, my lord; or if—I know not what.

OTHELLO.

Was not that Cassio parted from my wife?

IAGO.

Cassio, my lord? No, sure, I cannot think it,

That he would steal away so guilty-like,

Seeing you coming.

OTHELLO.

I do believe 'twas he.

DESDEMONA.

How now, my lord?

I have been talking with a suitor here,

A man that languishes in your displeasure.

OTHELLO.

Who is't you mean?

DESDEMONA.

Why, your lieutenant, Cassio. Good my lord,

If I have any grace or power to move you,

His present reconciliation take;

For if he be not one that truly loves you,

That errs in ignorance and not in cunning,

I have no judgement in an honest face.

I prithee call him back.

OTHELLO.

Went he hence now?

DESDEMONA.

Ay, sooth; so humbled

That he hath left part of his grief with me

To suffer with him. Good love, call him back.

OTHELLO.

Not now, sweet Desdemon, some other time.

DESDEMONA.

But shall't be shortly?

OTHELLO.

The sooner, sweet, for you.

DESDEMONA.

Shall't be tonight at supper?

OTHELLO.

No, not tonight.

DESDEMONA.

Tomorrow dinner then?

OTHELLO.

I shall not dine at home;

I meet the captains at the citadel.

DESDEMONA.

Why then tomorrow night, or Tuesday morn,

On Tuesday noon, or night; on Wednesday morn.

I prithee name the time, but let it not

Exceed three days. In faith, he's penitent;

And yet his trespass, in our common reason,

(Save that, they say, the wars must make examples

Out of their best) is not almost a fault

To incur a private check. When shall he come?

Tell me, Othello: I wonder in my soul,

What you would ask me, that I should deny,

Or stand so mammering on. What? Michael Cassio,

That came a-wooing with you, and so many a time,

When I have spoke of you dispraisingly,

Hath ta'en your part, to have so much to do

To bring him in! Trust me, I could do much.

OTHELLO.

Prithee no more. Let him come when he will;

I will deny thee nothing.

DESDEMONA.

Why, this is not a boon;

'Tis as I should entreat you wear your gloves,

Or feed on nourishing dishes, or keep you warm,

Or sue to you to do a peculiar profit

To your own person: nay, when I have a suit

Wherein I mean to touch your love indeed,

It shall be full of poise and difficult weight,

And fearful to be granted.

OTHELLO.

I will deny thee nothing.

Whereon, I do beseech thee, grant me this,

To leave me but a little to myself.

DESDEMONA.

Shall I deny you? No, farewell, my lord.

OTHELLO.

Farewell, my Desdemona. I'll come to thee straight.

DESDEMONA.

Emilia, come. Be as your fancies teach you.

Whate'er you be, I am obedient.

[Exit with Emilia.]

OTHELLO.

Excellent wretch! Perdition catch my soul,

But I do love thee! And when I love thee not,

Chaos is come again.

IAGO.

My noble lord,—

OTHELLO.

What dost thou say, Iago?

IAGO.

Did Michael Cassio, when you woo'd my lady,

Know of your love?

OTHELLO.

He did, from first to last. Why dost thou ask?

IAGO.

But for a satisfaction of my thought.

No further harm.

OTHELLO.

Why of thy thought, Iago?

IAGO.

I did not think he had been acquainted with her.

OTHELLO.

O yes, and went between us very oft.

IAGO.

Indeed?

OTHELLO.

Indeed? Ay, indeed. Discern'st thou aught in that?

Is he not honest?

IAGO.

Honest, my lord?

OTHELLO.

Honest? ay, honest.

IAGO.

My lord, for aught I know.

OTHELLO.

What dost thou think?

IAGO.

Think, my lord?

OTHELLO.

Think, my lord? By heaven, he echoes me,

As if there were some monster in his thought

Too hideous to be shown. Thou dost mean something.

I heard thee say even now, thou lik'st not that,

When Cassio left my wife. What didst not like?

And when I told thee he was of my counsel

In my whole course of wooing, thou criedst, "Indeed?"

And didst contract and purse thy brow together,

As if thou then hadst shut up in thy brain

Some horrible conceit: if thou dost love me,

Show me thy thought.

IAGO.

My lord, you know I love you.

OTHELLO.

I think thou dost;

And for I know thou'rt full of love and honesty

And weigh'st thy words before thou giv'st them breath,

Therefore these stops of thine fright me the more:

For such things in a false disloyal knave

Are tricks of custom; but in a man that's just,

They're close dilations, working from the heart,

That passion cannot rule.

IAGO.

For Michael Cassio,

I dare be sworn I think that he is honest.

OTHELLO.

I think so too.

IAGO.

Men should be what they seem;

Or those that be not, would they might seem none!

OTHELLO.

Certain, men should be what they seem.

IAGO.

Why then, I think Cassio's an honest man.

OTHELLO.

Nay, yet there's more in this:

I prithee, speak to me as to thy thinkings,

As thou dost ruminate, and give thy worst of thoughts

The worst of words.

IAGO.

Good my lord, pardon me.

Though I am bound to every act of duty,

I am not bound to that all slaves are free to.

Utter my thoughts? Why, say they are vile and false:

As where's that palace whereinto foul things

Sometimes intrude not? Who has a breast so pure

But some uncleanly apprehensions

Keep leets and law-days, and in session sit

With meditations lawful?

OTHELLO.

Thou dost conspire against thy friend, Iago,

If thou but think'st him wrong'd and mak'st his ear

A stranger to thy thoughts.

IAGO.

I do beseech you,

Though I perchance am vicious in my guess,

As, I confess, it is my nature's plague

To spy into abuses, and of my jealousy

Shapes faults that are not,—that your wisdom

From one that so imperfectly conceits,

Would take no notice; nor build yourself a trouble

Out of his scattering and unsure observance.

It were not for your quiet nor your good,

Nor for my manhood, honesty, or wisdom,

To let you know my thoughts.

OTHELLO.

What dost thou mean?

IAGO.

Good name in man and woman, dear my lord,

Is the immediate jewel of their souls.

Who steals my purse steals trash. 'Tis something, nothing;

'Twas mine, 'tis his, and has been slave to thousands.

But he that filches from me my good name

Robs me of that which not enriches him

And makes me poor indeed.

OTHELLO.

By heaven, I'll know thy thoughts.

IAGO.

You cannot, if my heart were in your hand,

Nor shall not, whilst 'tis in my custody.

OTHELLO.

Ha?

IAGO.

O, beware, my lord, of jealousy;

It is the green-ey'd monster which doth mock

The meat it feeds on. That cuckold lives in bliss

Who, certain of his fate, loves not his wronger;

But O, what damned minutes tells he o'er

Who dotes, yet doubts, suspects, yet strongly loves!

OTHELLO.

O misery!

IAGO.

Poor and content is rich, and rich enough;

But riches fineless is as poor as winter

To him that ever fears he shall be poor.

Good heaven, the souls of all my tribe defend

From jealousy!

OTHELLO.

Why, why is this?

Think'st thou I'd make a life of jealousy,

To follow still the changes of the moon

With fresh suspicions? No. To be once in doubt

Is once to be resolv'd: exchange me for a goat

When I shall turn the business of my soul

To such exsufflicate and blown surmises,

Matching thy inference. 'Tis not to make me jealous,

To say my wife is fair, feeds well, loves company,

Is free of speech, sings, plays, and dances well;

Where virtue is, these are more virtuous:

Nor from mine own weak merits will I draw

The smallest fear or doubt of her revolt,

For she had eyes, and chose me. No, Iago,

I'll see before I doubt; when I doubt, prove;

And on the proof, there is no more but this:

Away at once with love or jealousy!

IAGO.

I am glad of it, for now I shall have reason

To show the love and duty that I bear you

With franker spirit: therefore, as I am bound,

Receive it from me. I speak not yet of proof.

Look to your wife; observe her well with Cassio;

Wear your eye thus, not jealous nor secure.

I would not have your free and noble nature,

Out of self-bounty, be abus'd. Look to't.

I know our country disposition well;

In Venice they do let heaven see the pranks

They dare not show their husbands. Their best conscience

Is not to leave undone, but keep unknown.

OTHELLO.

Dost thou say so?

IAGO.

She did deceive her father, marrying you;

And when she seem'd to shake and fear your looks,

She loved them most.

OTHELLO.

And so she did.

IAGO.

Why, go to then.

She that so young could give out such a seeming,

To seal her father's eyes up close as oak,

He thought 'twas witchcraft. But I am much to blame.

I humbly do beseech you of your pardon

For too much loving you.

OTHELLO.

I am bound to thee for ever.

IAGO.

I see this hath a little dash'd your spirits.

OTHELLO.

Not a jot, not a jot.

IAGO.

Trust me, I fear it has.

I hope you will consider what is spoke

Comes from my love. But I do see you're mov'd.

I am to pray you not to strain my speech

To grosser issues nor to larger reach

Than to suspicion.

OTHELLO.

I will not.

IAGO.

Should you do so, my lord,

My speech should fall into such vile success

Which my thoughts aim'd not. Cassio's my worthy friend.

My lord, I see you're mov'd.

OTHELLO.

No, not much mov'd.

I do not think but Desdemona's honest.

IAGO.

Long live she so! And long live you to think so!

OTHELLO.

And yet, how nature erring from itself—

IAGO.

Ay, there's the point. As, to be bold with you,

Not to affect many proposed matches,

Of her own clime, complexion, and degree,

Whereto we see in all things nature tends;

Foh! One may smell in such a will most rank,

Foul disproportion, thoughts unnatural.

But pardon me: I do not in position

Distinctly speak of her, though I may fear

Her will, recoiling to her better judgement,

May fall to match you with her country forms,

And happily repent.

OTHELLO.

Farewell, farewell:

If more thou dost perceive, let me know more;

Set on thy wife to observe. Leave me, Iago.

IAGO.

[Going.] My lord, I take my leave.

OTHELLO.

Why did I marry? This honest creature doubtless

Sees and knows more, much more, than he unfolds.

IAGO.

[Returning.] My lord, I would I might entreat your honour

To scan this thing no further. Leave it to time:

Though it be fit that Cassio have his place,

For sure he fills it up with great ability,

Yet if you please to hold him off awhile,

You shall by that perceive him and his means.

Note if your lady strain his entertainment

With any strong or vehement importunity,

Much will be seen in that. In the meantime,

Let me be thought too busy in my fears

(As worthy cause I have to fear I am)

And hold her free, I do beseech your honour.

OTHELLO.

Fear not my government.

IAGO.

I once more take my leave.

[Exit.]

OTHELLO.

This fellow's of exceeding honesty,

And knows all qualities, with a learned spirit,

Of human dealings. If I do prove her haggard,

Though that her jesses were my dear heartstrings,

I'd whistle her off, and let her down the wind

109

To prey at fortune. Haply, for I am black,

And have not those soft parts of conversation

That chamberers have, or for I am declin'd

Into the vale of years,—yet that's not much—

She's gone, I am abus'd, and my relief

Must be to loathe her. O curse of marriage,

That we can call these delicate creatures ours,

And not their appetites! I had rather be a toad,

And live upon the vapour of a dungeon,

Than keep a corner in the thing I love

For others' uses. Yet, 'tis the plague of great ones,

Prerogativ'd are they less than the base,

'Tis destiny unshunnable, like death:

Even then this forked plague is fated to us

When we do quicken. Desdemona comes.

If she be false, O, then heaven mocks itself!

I'll not believe't.

Enter Desdemona and Emilia.

DESDEMONA.

How now, my dear Othello?

Your dinner, and the generous islanders

By you invited, do attend your presence.

OTHELLO.

I am to blame.

DESDEMONA.

Why do you speak so faintly?

Are you not well?

OTHELLO.

I have a pain upon my forehead here.

DESDEMONA.

Faith, that's with watching, 'twill away again;

Let me but bind it hard, within this hour

It will be well.

OTHELLO.

Your napkin is too little;

        [He puts the handkerchief from him, and she drops it.]

Let it alone. Come, I'll go in with you.

DESDEMONA.

I am very sorry that you are not well.

        [Exeunt Othello and Desdemona.]

EMILIA.

I am glad I have found this napkin;

This was her first remembrance from the Moor.

My wayward husband hath a hundred times

Woo'd me to steal it. But she so loves the token,

For he conjur'd her she should ever keep it,

That she reserves it evermore about her

To kiss and talk to. I'll have the work ta'en out,

And give't Iago. What he will do with it

Heaven knows, not I,

I nothing but to please his fantasy.

Enter Iago.

IAGO.

How now? What do you here alone?

EMILIA.

Do not you chide. I have a thing for you.

IAGO.

A thing for me? It is a common thing—

EMILIA.

Ha?

IAGO.

To have a foolish wife.

EMILIA.

O, is that all? What will you give me now

For that same handkerchief?

IAGO.

What handkerchief?

EMILIA.

What handkerchief?

Why, that the Moor first gave to Desdemona,

That which so often you did bid me steal.

IAGO.

Hast stol'n it from her?

EMILIA.

No, faith, she let it drop by negligence,

And, to the advantage, I being here, took 't up.

Look, here it is.

IAGO.

A good wench, give it me.

EMILIA.

What will you do with't, that you have been so earnest

To have me filch it?

IAGO.

[Snatching it.] Why, what's that to you?

EMILIA.

If it be not for some purpose of import,

Give 't me again. Poor lady, she'll run mad

When she shall lack it.

IAGO.

Be not acknown on't, I have use for it.

Go, leave me.

[Exit Emilia.]

I will in Cassio's lodging lose this napkin,

And let him find it. Trifles light as air

Are to the jealous confirmations strong

As proofs of holy writ. This may do something.

The Moor already changes with my poison:

Dangerous conceits are in their natures poisons,

Which at the first are scarce found to distaste,

But with a little act upon the blood

Burn like the mines of sulphur. I did say so.

Enter Othello.

Look, where he comes. Not poppy, nor mandragora,

Nor all the drowsy syrups of the world,

Shall ever medicine thee to that sweet sleep

Which thou ow'dst yesterday.

OTHELLO.

Ha! ha! false to me?

IAGO.

Why, how now, general? No more of that.

OTHELLO.

Avaunt! be gone! Thou hast set me on the rack.

I swear 'tis better to be much abus'd

Than but to know't a little.

IAGO.

How now, my lord?

OTHELLO.

What sense had I of her stol'n hours of lust?

I saw't not, thought it not, it harm'd not me.

I slept the next night well, was free and merry;

I found not Cassio's kisses on her lips.

He that is robb'd, not wanting what is stol'n,

Let him not know't, and he's not robb'd at all.

IAGO.

I am sorry to hear this.

OTHELLO.

I had been happy if the general camp,

Pioners and all, had tasted her sweet body,

So I had nothing known. O, now, for ever

Farewell the tranquil mind! Farewell content!

Farewell the plumed troops and the big wars

That make ambition virtue! O, farewell,

Farewell the neighing steed and the shrill trump,

The spirit-stirring drum, the ear-piercing fife,

The royal banner, and all quality,

Pride, pomp, and circumstance of glorious war!

And, O you mortal engines, whose rude throats

The immortal Jove's dread clamours counterfeit,

Farewell! Othello's occupation's gone!

IAGO.

Is't possible, my lord?

OTHELLO.

Villain, be sure thou prove my love a whore;

Be sure of it. Give me the ocular proof,

Or, by the worth of man's eternal soul,

Thou hadst been better have been born a dog

Than answer my wak'd wrath.

IAGO.

Is't come to this?

OTHELLO.

Make me to see't, or at the least so prove it,

That the probation bear no hinge nor loop

To hang a doubt on, or woe upon thy life!

IAGO.

My noble lord,—

OTHELLO.

If thou dost slander her and torture me,

Never pray more. Abandon all remorse;

On horror's head horrors accumulate;

Do deeds to make heaven weep, all earth amaz'd;

For nothing canst thou to damnation add

Greater than that.

IAGO.

O grace! O heaven defend me!

Are you a man? Have you a soul or sense?

God be wi' you. Take mine office.—O wretched fool,

That liv'st to make thine honesty a vice!

O monstrous world! Take note, take note, O world,

To be direct and honest is not safe.

I thank you for this profit, and from hence

I'll love no friend, sith love breeds such offence.

OTHELLO.

Nay, stay. Thou shouldst be honest.

IAGO.

I should be wise; for honesty's a fool,

And loses that it works for.

OTHELLO.

By the world,

I think my wife be honest, and think she is not.

I think that thou art just, and think thou art not.

I'll have some proof: her name, that was as fresh

As Dian's visage, is now begrim'd and black

As mine own face. If there be cords or knives,

Poison or fire, or suffocating streams,

I'll not endure 't. Would I were satisfied!

IAGO.

I see, sir, you are eaten up with passion.

I do repent me that I put it to you.

You would be satisfied?

OTHELLO.

Would? Nay, I will.

IAGO.

And may; but how? How satisfied, my lord?

Would you, the supervisor, grossly gape on,

Behold her topp'd?

OTHELLO.

Death and damnation! O!

IAGO.

It were a tedious difficulty, I think,

To bring them to that prospect. Damn them then,

If ever mortal eyes do see them bolster

More than their own! What then? How then?

What shall I say? Where's satisfaction?

It is impossible you should see this,

Were they as prime as goats, as hot as monkeys,

As salt as wolves in pride, and fools as gross

As ignorance made drunk. But yet I say,

If imputation and strong circumstances,

Which lead directly to the door of truth,

Will give you satisfaction, you may have't.

OTHELLO.

Give me a living reason she's disloyal.

IAGO.

I do not like the office,

But sith I am enter'd in this cause so far,

Prick'd to 't by foolish honesty and love,

I will go on. I lay with Cassio lately,

And being troubled with a raging tooth,

I could not sleep.

There are a kind of men so loose of soul,

That in their sleeps will mutter their affairs.

One of this kind is Cassio:

In sleep I heard him say, "Sweet Desdemona,

Let us be wary, let us hide our loves;"

And then, sir, would he gripe and wring my hand,

Cry "O sweet creature!" and then kiss me hard,

As if he pluck'd up kisses by the roots,

That grew upon my lips, then laid his leg

Over my thigh, and sigh'd and kiss'd, and then

Cried "Cursed fate that gave thee to the Moor!"

OTHELLO.

O monstrous! monstrous!

IAGO.

Nay, this was but his dream.

OTHELLO.

But this denoted a foregone conclusion.

'Tis a shrewd doubt, though it be but a dream.

IAGO.

And this may help to thicken other proofs

That do demonstrate thinly.

OTHELLO.

I'll tear her all to pieces.

IAGO.

Nay, but be wise. Yet we see nothing done,

She may be honest yet. Tell me but this,

Have you not sometimes seen a handkerchief

Spotted with strawberries in your wife's hand?

OTHELLO.

I gave her such a one, 'twas my first gift.

IAGO.

I know not that: but such a handkerchief

(I am sure it was your wife's) did I today

See Cassio wipe his beard with.

OTHELLO.

If it be that,—

IAGO.

If it be that, or any that was hers,

It speaks against her with the other proofs.

OTHELLO.

O, that the slave had forty thousand lives!

One is too poor, too weak for my revenge!

Now do I see 'tis true. Look here, Iago;

All my fond love thus do I blow to heaven.

'Tis gone.

Arise, black vengeance, from thy hollow hell!

Yield up, O love, thy crown and hearted throne

To tyrannous hate! Swell, bosom, with thy fraught,

For 'tis of aspics' tongues!

IAGO.

Yet be content.

OTHELLO.

O, blood, Iago, blood!

IAGO.

Patience, I say. Your mind perhaps may change.

OTHELLO.

Never, Iago. Like to the Pontic Sea,

Whose icy current and compulsive course

Ne'er feels retiring ebb, but keeps due on

To the Propontic and the Hellespont;

Even so my bloody thoughts, with violent pace

Shall ne'er look back, ne'er ebb to humble love,

Till that a capable and wide revenge

Swallow them up. Now by yond marble heaven,

In the due reverence of a sacred vow [Kneels.]

I here engage my words.

IAGO.

Do not rise yet. [Kneels.]

Witness, you ever-burning lights above,

You elements that clip us round about,

Witness that here Iago doth give up

The execution of his wit, hands, heart,

To wrong'd Othello's service! Let him command,

And to obey shall be in me remorse,

What bloody business ever.

[They rise.]

OTHELLO.

I greet thy love,

Not with vain thanks, but with acceptance bounteous,

And will upon the instant put thee to 't.

Within these three days let me hear thee say

That Cassio's not alive.

IAGO.

My friend is dead. 'Tis done at your request.

But let her live.

OTHELLO.

Damn her, lewd minx! O, damn her, damn her!

Come, go with me apart, I will withdraw

To furnish me with some swift means of death

For the fair devil. Now art thou my lieutenant.

IAGO.

I am your own for ever.

[Exeunt.]

SCENE IV. Cyprus. Before the Castle.

Enter Desdemona, Emilia and Clown.

DESDEMONA.

Do you know, sirrah, where Lieutenant Cassio lies?

CLOWN.

I dare not say he lies anywhere.

DESDEMONA.

Why, man?

CLOWN.

He's a soldier; and for one to say a soldier lies is stabbing.

DESDEMONA.

Go to. Where lodges he?

CLOWN.

To tell you where he lodges is to tell you where I lie.

DESDEMONA.

Can anything be made of this?

CLOWN.

I know not where he lodges; and for me to devise a lodging, and say he lies here, or he lies there, were to lie in mine own throat.

DESDEMONA.

Can you inquire him out, and be edified by report?

CLOWN.

I will catechize the world for him, that is, make questions and by them answer.

DESDEMONA.

Seek him, bid him come hither. Tell him I have moved my lord on his behalf, and hope all will be well.

CLOWN.

To do this is within the compass of man's wit, and therefore I will attempt the doing it.

[Exit.]

DESDEMONA.

Where should I lose that handkerchief, Emilia?

EMILIA.

I know not, madam.

DESDEMONA.

Believe me, I had rather have lost my purse

Full of crusadoes. And but my noble Moor

Is true of mind and made of no such baseness

As jealous creatures are, it were enough

To put him to ill thinking.

EMILIA.

Is he not jealous?

DESDEMONA.

Who, he? I think the sun where he was born

Drew all such humours from him.

EMILIA.

Look, where he comes.

Enter Othello.

DESDEMONA.

I will not leave him now till Cassio

Be call'd to him. How is't with you, my lord?

OTHELLO.

Well, my good lady. [Aside.] O, hardness to dissemble!

How do you, Desdemona?

DESDEMONA.

Well, my good lord.

OTHELLO.

Give me your hand. This hand is moist, my lady.

DESDEMONA.

It yet hath felt no age nor known no sorrow.

OTHELLO.

This argues fruitfulness and liberal heart.

Hot, hot, and moist. This hand of yours requires

A sequester from liberty, fasting and prayer,

Much castigation, exercise devout;

For here's a young and sweating devil here

That commonly rebels. 'Tis a good hand,

A frank one.

DESDEMONA.

You may indeed say so,

For 'twas that hand that gave away my heart.

OTHELLO.

A liberal hand. The hearts of old gave hands,

But our new heraldry is hands, not hearts.

DESDEMONA.

I cannot speak of this. Come now, your promise.

OTHELLO.

What promise, chuck?

DESDEMONA.

I have sent to bid Cassio come speak with you.

OTHELLO.

I have a salt and sorry rheum offends me.

Lend me thy handkerchief.

DESDEMONA.

Here, my lord.

OTHELLO.

That which I gave you.

DESDEMONA.

I have it not about me.

OTHELLO.

Not?

DESDEMONA.

No, faith, my lord.

OTHELLO.

That is a fault. That handkerchief

Did an Egyptian to my mother give.

She was a charmer, and could almost read

The thoughts of people. She told her, while she kept it,

'Twould make her amiable and subdue my father

Entirely to her love. But if she lost it,

Or made a gift of it, my father's eye

Should hold her loathed, and his spirits should hunt

After new fancies: she, dying, gave it me,

And bid me, when my fate would have me wive,

To give it her. I did so; and take heed on't,

Make it a darling like your precious eye.

To lose't or give't away were such perdition

As nothing else could match.

DESDEMONA.

Is't possible?

OTHELLO.

'Tis true. There's magic in the web of it.

A sibyl, that had number'd in the world

The sun to course two hundred compasses,

In her prophetic fury sew'd the work;

The worms were hallow'd that did breed the silk,

And it was dyed in mummy, which the skillful

Conserv'd of maiden's hearts.

DESDEMONA.

Indeed? Is't true?

OTHELLO.

Most veritable, therefore look to 't well.

DESDEMONA.

Then would to God that I had never seen 't!

OTHELLO.

Ha? wherefore?

DESDEMONA.

Why do you speak so startingly and rash?

OTHELLO.

Is't lost? is't gone? speak, is it out of the way?

DESDEMONA.

Heaven bless us!

OTHELLO.

Say you?

DESDEMONA.

It is not lost, but what and if it were?

OTHELLO.

How?

DESDEMONA.

I say it is not lost.

OTHELLO.

Fetch't, let me see 't.

DESDEMONA.

Why, so I can, sir, but I will not now.

This is a trick to put me from my suit.

Pray you, let Cassio be receiv'd again.

OTHELLO.

Fetch me the handkerchief! My mind misgives.

DESDEMONA.

Come, come.

You'll never meet a more sufficient man.

OTHELLO.

The handkerchief!

DESDEMONA.

I pray, talk me of Cassio.

OTHELLO.

The handkerchief!

DESDEMONA.

A man that all his time

Hath founded his good fortunes on your love,

Shar'd dangers with you,—

OTHELLO.

The handkerchief!

DESDEMONA.

In sooth, you are to blame.

OTHELLO.

Away!

[Exit.]

EMILIA.

Is not this man jealous?

DESDEMONA.

I ne'er saw this before.

Sure there's some wonder in this handkerchief,

I am most unhappy in the loss of it.

EMILIA.

'Tis not a year or two shows us a man:

They are all but stomachs and we all but food;

They eat us hungerly, and when they are full,

They belch us.

Enter Cassio and Iago.

Look you, Cassio and my husband.

IAGO.

There is no other way; 'tis she must do 't,

And, lo, the happiness! Go and importune her.

DESDEMONA.

How now, good Cassio, what's the news with you?

131

CASSIO.

Madam, my former suit: I do beseech you

That by your virtuous means I may again

Exist, and be a member of his love,

Whom I, with all the office of my heart,

Entirely honour. I would not be delay'd.

If my offence be of such mortal kind

That nor my service past, nor present sorrows,

Nor purpos'd merit in futurity,

Can ransom me into his love again,

But to know so must be my benefit;

So shall I clothe me in a forc'd content,

And shut myself up in some other course

To fortune's alms.

DESDEMONA.

Alas, thrice-gentle Cassio,

My advocation is not now in tune;

My lord is not my lord; nor should I know him

Were he in favour as in humour alter'd.

So help me every spirit sanctified,

As I have spoken for you all my best,

And stood within the blank of his displeasure

For my free speech! You must awhile be patient.

What I can do I will; and more I will

Than for myself I dare. Let that suffice you.

IAGO.

Is my lord angry?

EMILIA.

He went hence but now,

And certainly in strange unquietness.

IAGO.

Can he be angry? I have seen the cannon,

When it hath blown his ranks into the air

And, like the devil, from his very arm

Puff'd his own brother, and can he be angry?

Something of moment then. I will go meet him.

There's matter in't indeed if he be angry.

DESDEMONA.

I prithee do so.

[Exit Iago.]

Something sure of state,

Either from Venice, or some unhatch'd practice

Made demonstrable here in Cyprus to him,

Hath puddled his clear spirit, and in such cases

Men's natures wrangle with inferior things,

Though great ones are their object. 'Tis even so.

For let our finger ache, and it indues

Our other healthful members even to that sense

Of pain. Nay, we must think men are not gods,

Nor of them look for such observancy

As fits the bridal. Beshrew me much, Emilia,

I was (unhandsome warrior as I am)

Arraigning his unkindness with my soul;

But now I find I had suborn'd the witness,

And he's indicted falsely.

EMILIA.

Pray heaven it be state matters, as you think,

And no conception nor no jealous toy

Concerning you.

DESDEMONA.

Alas the day, I never gave him cause!

EMILIA.

But jealous souls will not be answer'd so;

They are not ever jealous for the cause,

But jealous for they are jealous: 'tis a monster

Begot upon itself, born on itself.

DESDEMONA.

Heaven keep that monster from Othello's mind!

EMILIA.

Lady, amen.

DESDEMONA.

I will go seek him. Cassio, walk hereabout:

If I do find him fit, I'll move your suit,

And seek to effect it to my uttermost.

CASSIO.

I humbly thank your ladyship.

[Exeunt Desdemona and Emilia.]

Enter Bianca.

BIANCA.

Save you, friend Cassio!

CASSIO.

What make you from home?

How is it with you, my most fair Bianca?

I' faith, sweet love, I was coming to your house.

BIANCA.

And I was going to your lodging, Cassio.

What, keep a week away? Seven days and nights?

Eight score eight hours, and lovers' absent hours,

More tedious than the dial eight score times?

O weary reckoning!

CASSIO.

Pardon me, Bianca.

I have this while with leaden thoughts been press'd,

But I shall in a more continuate time

Strike off this score of absence. Sweet Bianca,

[Giving her Desdemona's handkerchief.]

Take me this work out.

BIANCA.

O Cassio, whence came this?

This is some token from a newer friend.

To the felt absence now I feel a cause.

Is't come to this? Well, well.

CASSIO.

Go to, woman!

Throw your vile guesses in the devil's teeth,

From whence you have them. You are jealous now

That this is from some mistress, some remembrance.

No, in good troth, Bianca.

BIANCA.

Why, whose is it?

CASSIO.

I know not neither. I found it in my chamber.

I like the work well. Ere it be demanded,

As like enough it will, I'd have it copied.

Take it, and do 't, and leave me for this time.

BIANCA.

Leave you, wherefore?

CASSIO.

I do attend here on the general,

And think it no addition, nor my wish,

To have him see me woman'd.

BIANCA.

Why, I pray you?

CASSIO.

Not that I love you not.

BIANCA.

But that you do not love me.

I pray you bring me on the way a little,

And say if I shall see you soon at night.

CASSIO.

'Tis but a little way that I can bring you,

For I attend here. But I'll see you soon.

BIANCA.

'Tis very good; I must be circumstanc'd.

[Exeunt.]

ACT IV

SCENE I. Cyprus. Before the Castle.

Enter Othello and Iago.

IAGO.

Will you think so?

OTHELLO.

Think so, Iago?

IAGO.

What,

To kiss in private?

OTHELLO.

An unauthoriz'd kiss.

IAGO.

Or to be naked with her friend in bed

An hour or more, not meaning any harm?

OTHELLO.

Naked in bed, Iago, and not mean harm?

It is hypocrisy against the devil:

They that mean virtuously and yet do so,

The devil their virtue tempts, and they tempt heaven.

IAGO.

So they do nothing, 'tis a venial slip.

But if I give my wife a handkerchief—

OTHELLO.

What then?

IAGO.

Why then, 'tis hers, my lord, and being hers,

She may, I think, bestow't on any man.

OTHELLO.

She is protectress of her honour too.

May she give that?

IAGO.

Her honour is an essence that's not seen;

They have it very oft that have it not:

But for the handkerchief—

OTHELLO.

By heaven, I would most gladly have forgot it.

Thou said'st (O, it comes o'er my memory,

As doth the raven o'er the infected house,

Boding to all) he had my handkerchief.

IAGO.

Ay, what of that?

OTHELLO.

That's not so good now.

IAGO.

What

If I had said I had seen him do you wrong?

Or heard him say (as knaves be such abroad,

Who having, by their own importunate suit,

Or voluntary dotage of some mistress,

Convinced or supplied them, cannot choose

But they must blab.)

OTHELLO.

Hath he said anything?

IAGO.

He hath, my lord, but be you well assur'd,

No more than he'll unswear.

OTHELLO.

What hath he said?

IAGO.

Faith, that he did—I know not what he did.

OTHELLO.

What? What?

IAGO.

Lie.

OTHELLO.

With her?

IAGO.

With her, on her, what you will.

OTHELLO.

Lie with her! lie on her!—We say lie on her when they belie her.—
Lie with her! that's fulsome. Handkerchief—confessions—handkerchief!
To confess, and be hanged for his labour. First, to be hanged, and then to
confess. I tremble at it. Nature would not invest herself in such shadowing
passion without some instruction. It is not words that shake me thus. Pish!
Noses, ears, and lips. Is't possible?—Confess?—handkerchief?—O devil!—

[Falls in a trance.]

IAGO.

Work on,

My medicine, work! Thus credulous fools are caught,

And many worthy and chaste dames even thus,

All guiltless, meet reproach. What, ho! my lord!

My lord, I say! Othello!

Enter Cassio.

How now, Cassio!

CASSIO.

What's the matter?

IAGO.

My lord is fallen into an epilepsy.

This is his second fit. He had one yesterday.

CASSIO.

Rub him about the temples.

IAGO.

No, forbear;

The lethargy must have his quiet course.

If not, he foams at mouth, and by and by

Breaks out to savage madness. Look, he stirs:

Do you withdraw yourself a little while,

He will recover straight. When he is gone,

I would on great occasion speak with you.

[Exit Cassio.]

How is it, general? Have you not hurt your head?

OTHELLO.

Dost thou mock me?

IAGO.

I mock you? No, by heaven.

Would you would bear your fortune like a man!

OTHELLO.

A horned man's a monster and a beast.

IAGO.

There's many a beast, then, in a populous city,

And many a civil monster.

OTHELLO.

Did he confess it?

IAGO.

Good sir, be a man.

Think every bearded fellow that's but yok'd

May draw with you. There's millions now alive

That nightly lie in those unproper beds

Which they dare swear peculiar: your case is better.

O, 'tis the spite of hell, the fiend's arch-mock,

To lip a wanton in a secure couch,

And to suppose her chaste! No, let me know,

And knowing what I am, I know what she shall be.

OTHELLO.

O, thou art wise, 'tis certain.

IAGO.

Stand you awhile apart,

Confine yourself but in a patient list.

Whilst you were here o'erwhelmed with your grief,

(A passion most unsuiting such a man)

Cassio came hither. I shifted him away,

And laid good 'scuse upon your ecstasy,

Bade him anon return, and here speak with me,

The which he promis'd. Do but encave yourself,

And mark the fleers, the gibes, and notable scorns,

That dwell in every region of his face;

For I will make him tell the tale anew,

Where, how, how oft, how long ago, and when

He hath, and is again to cope your wife:

I say, but mark his gesture. Marry, patience,

Or I shall say you are all in all in spleen,

And nothing of a man.

OTHELLO.

Dost thou hear, Iago?

I will be found most cunning in my patience;

But,—dost thou hear?—most bloody.

IAGO.

That's not amiss.

But yet keep time in all. Will you withdraw?

[Othello withdraws.]

Now will I question Cassio of Bianca,

A housewife that by selling her desires

Buys herself bread and clothes: it is a creature

That dotes on Cassio, (as 'tis the strumpet's plague

To beguile many and be beguil'd by one.)

He, when he hears of her, cannot refrain

From the excess of laughter. Here he comes.

Enter Cassio.

As he shall smile Othello shall go mad,

And his unbookish jealousy must construe

Poor Cassio's smiles, gestures, and light behaviour

Quite in the wrong. How do you now, lieutenant?

CASSIO.

The worser that you give me the addition

Whose want even kills me.

IAGO.

Ply Desdemona well, and you are sure on't.

[Speaking lower.] Now, if this suit lay in Bianca's power,

How quickly should you speed!

CASSIO.

Alas, poor caitiff!

OTHELLO.

[Aside.] Look how he laughs already!

IAGO.

I never knew a woman love man so.

CASSIO.

Alas, poor rogue! I think, i' faith, she loves me.

OTHELLO.

[Aside.] Now he denies it faintly and laughs it out.

IAGO.

Do you hear, Cassio?

OTHELLO.

Now he importunes him

To tell it o'er. Go to, well said, well said.

IAGO.

She gives it out that you shall marry her.

Do you intend it?

CASSIO.

Ha, ha, ha!

OTHELLO.

Do you triumph, Roman? Do you triumph?

CASSIO.

I marry her? What? A customer? I prithee, bear some charity to my wit, do not think it so unwholesome. Ha, ha, ha!

OTHELLO.

So, so, so, so. They laugh that wins.

IAGO.

Faith, the cry goes that you shall marry her.

CASSIO.

Prithee say true.

IAGO.

I am a very villain else.

OTHELLO.

Have you scored me? Well.

CASSIO.

This is the monkey's own giving out. She is persuaded I will marry her, out of her own love and flattery, not out of my promise.

OTHELLO.

Iago beckons me. Now he begins the story.

CASSIO.

She was here even now. She haunts me in every place. I was the other day talking on the sea-bank with certain Venetians, and thither comes the bauble, and falls thus about my neck.

OTHELLO.

Crying, "O dear Cassio!" as it were: his gesture imports it.

CASSIO.

So hangs, and lolls, and weeps upon me; so hales and pulls me. Ha, ha, ha!

OTHELLO.

Now he tells how she plucked him to my chamber. O, I see that nose of yours, but not that dog I shall throw it to.

CASSIO.

Well, I must leave her company.

IAGO.

Before me! look where she comes.

Enter Bianca.

CASSIO.

'Tis such another fitchew! Marry, a perfum'd one.

What do you mean by this haunting of me?

BIANCA.

Let the devil and his dam haunt you! What did you mean by that same handkerchief you gave me even now? I was a fine fool to take it. I must take out the work? A likely piece of work, that you should find it in your chamber and not know who left it there! This is some minx's token, and I must take out the work? There, give it your hobby-horse. Wheresoever you had it, I'll take out no work on't.

CASSIO.

How now, my sweet Bianca? How now, how now?

OTHELLO.

By heaven, that should be my handkerchief!

BIANCA.

If you'll come to supper tonight, you may. If you will not, come when you are next prepared for.

[Exit.]

IAGO.

After her, after her.

CASSIO.

Faith, I must; she'll rail in the street else.

IAGO.

Will you sup there?

CASSIO.

Faith, I intend so.

IAGO.

Well, I may chance to see you, for I would very fain speak with you.

CASSIO.

Prithee come, will you?

IAGO.

Go to; say no more.

[Exit Cassio.]

OTHELLO.

[Coming forward.] How shall I murder him, Iago?

IAGO.

Did you perceive how he laughed at his vice?

OTHELLO.

O Iago!

IAGO.

And did you see the handkerchief?

OTHELLO.

Was that mine?

IAGO.

Yours, by this hand: and to see how he prizes the foolish woman your wife! she gave it him, and he hath given it his whore.

OTHELLO.

I would have him nine years a-killing. A fine woman, a fair woman, a sweet woman!

IAGO.

Nay, you must forget that.

OTHELLO.

Ay, let her rot, and perish, and be damned tonight, for she shall not live. No, my heart is turned to stone; I strike it, and it hurts my hand. O, the world hath not a sweeter creature. She might lie by an emperor's side, and command him tasks.

IAGO.

Nay, that's not your way.

OTHELLO.

Hang her, I do but say what she is. So delicate with her needle, an admirable musician! O, she will sing the savageness out of a bear! Of so high and plenteous wit and invention!

IAGO.

She's the worse for all this.

OTHELLO.

O, a thousand, a thousand times: and then of so gentle a condition!

IAGO.

Ay, too gentle.

OTHELLO.

Nay, that's certain. But yet the pity of it, Iago! O Iago, the pity of it, Iago!

IAGO.

If you are so fond over her iniquity, give her patent to offend, for if it touch not you, it comes near nobody.

OTHELLO.

I will chop her into messes. Cuckold me!

IAGO.

O, 'tis foul in her.

OTHELLO.

With mine officer!

IAGO.

That's fouler.

OTHELLO.

Get me some poison, Iago; this night. I'll not expostulate with her, lest her body and beauty unprovide my mind again. This night, Iago.

IAGO.

Do it not with poison, strangle her in her bed, even the bed she hath contaminated.

OTHELLO.

Good, good. The justice of it pleases. Very good.

IAGO.

And for Cassio, let me be his undertaker. You shall hear more by midnight.

OTHELLO.

Excellent good. [A trumpet within.] What trumpet is that same?

Enter Lodovico, Desdemona and Attendant.

IAGO.

Something from Venice, sure. 'Tis Lodovico

Come from the duke. See, your wife is with him.

LODOVICO.

Save you, worthy general!

OTHELLO.

With all my heart, sir.

LODOVICO.

The duke and senators of Venice greet you.

[Gives him a packet.]

OTHELLO.

I kiss the instrument of their pleasures.

[Opens the packet and reads.]

DESDEMONA.

And what's the news, good cousin Lodovico?

IAGO.

I am very glad to see you, signior.

Welcome to Cyprus.

LODOVICO.

I thank you. How does Lieutenant Cassio?

IAGO.

Lives, sir.

DESDEMONA.

Cousin, there's fall'n between him and my lord

An unkind breach, but you shall make all well.

OTHELLO.

Are you sure of that?

DESDEMONA.

My lord?

OTHELLO.

[Reads.] "This fail you not to do, as you will—"

LODOVICO.

He did not call; he's busy in the paper.

Is there division 'twixt my lord and Cassio?

DESDEMONA.

A most unhappy one. I would do much

To atone them, for the love I bear to Cassio.

OTHELLO.

Fire and brimstone!

DESDEMONA.

My lord?

OTHELLO.

Are you wise?

DESDEMONA.

What, is he angry?

LODOVICO.

May be the letter mov'd him;

For, as I think, they do command him home,

Deputing Cassio in his government.

DESDEMONA.

Trust me, I am glad on't.

OTHELLO.

Indeed!

DESDEMONA.

My lord?

OTHELLO.

I am glad to see you mad.

DESDEMONA.

Why, sweet Othello?

OTHELLO.

Devil!

[Striking her.]

DESDEMONA.

I have not deserv'd this.

LODOVICO.

My lord, this would not be believ'd in Venice,

Though I should swear I saw't: 'tis very much.

Make her amends. She weeps.

OTHELLO.

O devil, devil!

If that the earth could teem with woman's tears,

Each drop she falls would prove a crocodile.

Out of my sight!

DESDEMONA.

I will not stay to offend you.

[Going.]

LODOVICO.

Truly, an obedient lady.

I do beseech your lordship, call her back.

OTHELLO.

Mistress!

DESDEMONA.

My lord?

OTHELLO.

What would you with her, sir?

LODOVICO.

Who, I, my lord?

OTHELLO.

Ay, you did wish that I would make her turn.

Sir, she can turn, and turn, and yet go on,

And turn again. And she can weep, sir, weep;

And she's obedient, as you say, obedient,

Very obedient. Proceed you in your tears.

Concerning this, sir,—O well-painted passion!

I am commanded home.—Get you away;

I'll send for you anon.—Sir, I obey the mandate,

And will return to Venice.—Hence, avaunt!

[Exit Desdemona.]

Cassio shall have my place. And, sir, tonight,

I do entreat that we may sup together.

You are welcome, sir, to Cyprus. Goats and monkeys!

[Exit.]

LODOVICO.

Is this the noble Moor, whom our full senate

Call all in all sufficient? Is this the nature

Whom passion could not shake? whose solid virtue

The shot of accident nor dart of chance

Could neither graze nor pierce?

IAGO.

He is much chang'd.

LODOVICO.

Are his wits safe? Is he not light of brain?

IAGO.

He's that he is. I may not breathe my censure

What he might be. If what he might he is not,

I would to heaven he were!

LODOVICO.

What, strike his wife?

IAGO.

Faith, that was not so well; yet would I knew

That stroke would prove the worst!

LODOVICO.

Is it his use?

Or did the letters work upon his blood,

And new-create this fault?

IAGO.

Alas, alas!

It is not honesty in me to speak

What I have seen and known. You shall observe him,

And his own courses will denote him so

That I may save my speech: do but go after,

And mark how he continues.

LODOVICO.

I am sorry that I am deceiv'd in him.

[Exeunt.]

SCENE II. Cyprus. A Room in the Castle.

Enter Othello and Emilia.

OTHELLO.

You have seen nothing, then?

EMILIA.

Nor ever heard, nor ever did suspect.

OTHELLO.

Yes, you have seen Cassio and she together.

EMILIA.

But then I saw no harm, and then I heard

Each syllable that breath made up between them.

OTHELLO.

What, did they never whisper?

EMILIA.

Never, my lord.

OTHELLO.

Nor send you out o' the way?

EMILIA.

Never.

OTHELLO.

To fetch her fan, her gloves, her mask, nor nothing?

EMILIA.

Never, my lord.

OTHELLO.

That's strange.

EMILIA.

I durst, my lord, to wager she is honest,

Lay down my soul at stake: if you think other,

Remove your thought, it doth abuse your bosom.

If any wretch have put this in your head,

Let heaven requite it with the serpent's curse,

For if she be not honest, chaste, and true,

There's no man happy. The purest of their wives

Is foul as slander.

OTHELLO.

Bid her come hither. Go.

[Exit Emilia.]

She says enough. Yet she's a simple bawd

That cannot say as much. This is a subtle whore,

A closet lock and key of villainous secrets.

And yet she'll kneel and pray. I have seen her do 't.

Enter Desdemona and Emilia.

DESDEMONA.

My lord, what is your will?

OTHELLO.

Pray, chuck, come hither.

DESDEMONA.

What is your pleasure?

OTHELLO.

Let me see your eyes.

Look in my face.

DESDEMONA.

What horrible fancy's this?

OTHELLO.

[To Emilia.] Some of your function, mistress,

Leave procreants alone, and shut the door.

Cough, or cry hem, if anybody come.

Your mystery, your mystery. Nay, dispatch.

[Exit Emilia.]

DESDEMONA.

Upon my knees, what doth your speech import?

I understand a fury in your words,

But not the words.

OTHELLO.

Why, what art thou?

DESDEMONA.

Your wife, my lord, your true and loyal wife.

OTHELLO.

Come, swear it, damn thyself,

Lest, being like one of heaven, the devils themselves

Should fear to seize thee. Therefore be double-damn'd.

Swear thou art honest.

DESDEMONA.

Heaven doth truly know it.

OTHELLO.

Heaven truly knows that thou art false as hell.

DESDEMONA.

To whom, my lord? With whom? How am I false?

OTHELLO.

O Desdemona, away! away! away!

DESDEMONA.

Alas the heavy day, why do you weep?

Am I the motive of these tears, my lord?

If haply you my father do suspect

An instrument of this your calling back,

Lay not your blame on me. If you have lost him,

Why, I have lost him too.

OTHELLO.

Had it pleas'd heaven

To try me with affliction, had they rain'd

All kinds of sores and shames on my bare head,

Steep'd me in poverty to the very lips,

Given to captivity me and my utmost hopes,

I should have found in some place of my soul

A drop of patience. But, alas, to make me

A fixed figure for the time of scorn

To point his slow unmoving finger at.

Yet could I bear that too, well, very well:

But there, where I have garner'd up my heart,

Where either I must live or bear no life,

The fountain from the which my current runs,

Or else dries up, to be discarded thence,

Or keep it as a cistern for foul toads

To knot and gender in!—turn thy complexion there,

Patience, thou young and rose-lipp'd cherubin,

Ay, there, look grim as hell!

DESDEMONA.

I hope my noble lord esteems me honest.

OTHELLO.

O, ay, as summer flies are in the shambles,

That quicken even with blowing. O thou weed,

Who art so lovely fair, and smell'st so sweet,

That the sense aches at thee,

Would thou hadst ne'er been born!

DESDEMONA.

Alas, what ignorant sin have I committed?

OTHELLO.

Was this fair paper, this most goodly book,

Made to write "whore" upon? What committed?

Committed! O thou public commoner!

I should make very forges of my cheeks,

That would to cinders burn up modesty,

Did I but speak thy deeds. What committed!

Heaven stops the nose at it, and the moon winks;

The bawdy wind, that kisses all it meets,

Is hush'd within the hollow mine of earth,

And will not hear it. What committed!

Impudent strumpet!

DESDEMONA.

By heaven, you do me wrong.

OTHELLO.

Are not you a strumpet?

DESDEMONA.

No, as I am a Christian:

If to preserve this vessel for my lord

From any other foul unlawful touch

Be not to be a strumpet, I am none.

OTHELLO.

What, not a whore?

DESDEMONA.

No, as I shall be sav'd.

OTHELLO.

Is't possible?

DESDEMONA.

O, heaven forgive us!

OTHELLO.

I cry you mercy then.

I took you for that cunning whore of Venice

That married with Othello.—You, mistress,

Enter Emilia.

That have the office opposite to Saint Peter,

And keeps the gate of hell. You, you, ay, you!

We have done our course; there's money for your pains.

I pray you turn the key, and keep our counsel.

[Exit.]

EMILIA.

Alas, what does this gentleman conceive?

How do you, madam? How do you, my good lady?

DESDEMONA.

Faith, half asleep.

EMILIA.

Good madam, what's the matter with my lord?

DESDEMONA.

With who?

EMILIA.

Why, with my lord, madam.

DESDEMONA.

Who is thy lord?

EMILIA.

He that is yours, sweet lady.

DESDEMONA.

I have none. Do not talk to me, Emilia,

I cannot weep, nor answer have I none

But what should go by water. Prithee, tonight

Lay on my bed my wedding sheets, remember,

And call thy husband hither.

EMILIA.

Here's a change indeed!

[Exit.]

DESDEMONA.

'Tis meet I should be us'd so, very meet.

How have I been behav'd, that he might stick

The small'st opinion on my least misuse?

Enter Iago and Emilia.

IAGO.

What is your pleasure, madam? How is't with you?

DESDEMONA.

I cannot tell. Those that do teach young babes

Do it with gentle means and easy tasks.

He might have chid me so, for, in good faith,

I am a child to chiding.

IAGO.

What's the matter, lady?

EMILIA.

Alas, Iago, my lord hath so bewhor'd her,

Thrown such despite and heavy terms upon her,

As true hearts cannot bear.

DESDEMONA.

Am I that name, Iago?

IAGO.

What name, fair lady?

DESDEMONA.

Such as she says my lord did say I was.

EMILIA.

He call'd her whore: a beggar in his drink

Could not have laid such terms upon his callet.

IAGO.

Why did he so?

DESDEMONA.

I do not know. I am sure I am none such.

IAGO.

Do not weep, do not weep: alas the day!

EMILIA.

Hath she forsook so many noble matches,

Her father, and her country, and her friends,

To be call'd whore? would it not make one weep?

DESDEMONA.

It is my wretched fortune.

IAGO.

Beshrew him for't!

How comes this trick upon him?

DESDEMONA.

Nay, heaven doth know.

EMILIA.

I will be hang'd, if some eternal villain,

Some busy and insinuating rogue,

Some cogging, cozening slave, to get some office,

Have not devis'd this slander. I'll be hang'd else.

IAGO.

Fie, there is no such man. It is impossible.

DESDEMONA.

If any such there be, heaven pardon him!

EMILIA.

A halter pardon him, and hell gnaw his bones!

Why should he call her whore? who keeps her company?

What place? what time? what form? what likelihood?

The Moor's abused by some most villainous knave,

Some base notorious knave, some scurvy fellow.

O heaven, that such companions thou'dst unfold,

And put in every honest hand a whip

To lash the rascals naked through the world

Even from the east to the west!

IAGO.

Speak within door.

EMILIA.

O, fie upon them! Some such squire he was

That turn'd your wit the seamy side without,

And made you to suspect me with the Moor.

IAGO.

You are a fool. Go to.

DESDEMONA.

Alas, Iago,

What shall I do to win my lord again?

Good friend, go to him. For by this light of heaven,

I know not how I lost him. Here I kneel.

If e'er my will did trespass 'gainst his love,

Either in discourse of thought or actual deed,

Or that mine eyes, mine ears, or any sense,

Delighted them in any other form,

Or that I do not yet, and ever did,

And ever will, (though he do shake me off

To beggarly divorcement) love him dearly,

Comfort forswear me! Unkindness may do much;

And his unkindness may defeat my life,

But never taint my love. I cannot say "whore,"

It does abhor me now I speak the word;

To do the act that might the addition earn

Not the world's mass of vanity could make me.

IAGO.

I pray you, be content. 'Tis but his humour.

The business of the state does him offence,

And he does chide with you.

DESDEMONA.

If 'twere no other,—

IAGO.

'Tis but so, I warrant.

[Trumpets within.]

Hark, how these instruments summon to supper.

The messengers of Venice stay the meat.

Go in, and weep not. All things shall be well.

[Exeunt Desdemona and Emilia.]

Enter Roderigo.

How now, Roderigo?

RODERIGO.

I do not find that thou dealest justly with me.

IAGO.

What in the contrary?

RODERIGO.

Every day thou daffest me with some device, Iago, and rather, as it seems to me now, keepest from me all conveniency than suppliest me with the least advantage of hope. I will indeed no longer endure it. Nor am I yet persuaded to put up in peace what already I have foolishly suffered.

IAGO.

Will you hear me, Roderigo?

RODERIGO.

Faith, I have heard too much, for your words and performances are no kin together.

IAGO.

You charge me most unjustly.

RODERIGO.

With naught but truth. I have wasted myself out of my means. The jewels you have had from me to deliver to Desdemona would half have corrupted a votarist: you have told me she hath received them, and returned me expectations and comforts of sudden respect and acquaintance, but I find none.

IAGO.

Well, go to, very well.

RODERIGO.

Very well, go to, I cannot go to, man, nor 'tis not very well. Nay, I say 'tis very scurvy, and begin to find myself fopped in it.

IAGO.

Very well.

RODERIGO.

I tell you 'tis not very well. I will make myself known to Desdemona. If she will return me my jewels, I will give over my suit and repent my unlawful solicitation. If not, assure yourself I will seek satisfaction of you.

IAGO.

You have said now.

RODERIGO.

Ay, and said nothing but what I protest intendment of doing.

IAGO.

Why, now I see there's mettle in thee, and even from this instant do build on thee a better opinion than ever before. Give me thy hand, Roderigo. Thou hast taken against me a most just exception, but yet I protest, I have dealt most directly in thy affair.

RODERIGO.

It hath not appeared.

IAGO.

I grant indeed it hath not appeared, and your suspicion is not without wit and judgement. But, Roderigo, if thou hast that in thee indeed, which I have greater reason to believe now than ever,—I mean purpose, courage, and valour,—this night show it. If thou the next night following enjoy not

171

Desdemona, take me from this world with treachery and devise engines for my life.

RODERIGO.

Well, what is it? Is it within reason and compass?

IAGO.

Sir, there is especial commission come from Venice to depute Cassio in Othello's place.

RODERIGO.

Is that true? Why then Othello and Desdemona return again to Venice.

IAGO.

O, no; he goes into Mauritania, and takes away with him the fair Desdemona, unless his abode be lingered here by some accident: wherein none can be so determinate as the removing of Cassio.

RODERIGO.

How do you mean "removing" of him?

IAGO.

Why, by making him uncapable of Othello's place: knocking out his brains.

RODERIGO.

And that you would have me to do?

IAGO.

Ay, if you dare do yourself a profit and a right. He sups tonight with a harlotry, and thither will I go to him. He knows not yet of his honourable fortune. If you will watch his going thence, which I will fashion to fall out between twelve and one, you may take him at your pleasure: I will be near to second your attempt, and he shall fall between us. Come, stand not amazed at it, but go along with me. I will show you such a necessity in his death that you shall think yourself bound to put it on him. It is now high supper-time, and the night grows to waste. About it.

RODERIGO.

I will hear further reason for this.

IAGO.

And you shall be satisfied.

[Exeunt.]

SCENE III. Cyprus. Another Room in the Castle.

Enter Othello, Lodovico, Desdemona, Emilia and Attendants.

LODOVICO.

I do beseech you, sir, trouble yourself no further.

OTHELLO.

O, pardon me; 'twill do me good to walk.

LODOVICO.

Madam, good night. I humbly thank your ladyship.

DESDEMONA.

Your honour is most welcome.

OTHELLO.

Will you walk, sir?—

O, Desdemona,—

DESDEMONA.

My lord?

OTHELLO.

Get you to bed on th' instant, I will be return'd forthwith. Dismiss your attendant there. Look 't be done.

DESDEMONA.

I will, my lord.

> [Exeunt Othello, Lodovico and Attendants.]

EMILIA.

How goes it now? He looks gentler than he did.

DESDEMONA.

He says he will return incontinent,

He hath commanded me to go to bed,

And bade me to dismiss you.

EMILIA.

Dismiss me?

DESDEMONA.

It was his bidding. Therefore, good Emilia,

Give me my nightly wearing, and adieu.

We must not now displease him.

EMILIA.

I would you had never seen him!

DESDEMONA.

So would not I. My love doth so approve him,

That even his stubbornness, his checks, his frowns,—

Prithee, unpin me,—have grace and favour in them.

EMILIA.

I have laid those sheets you bade me on the bed.

DESDEMONA.

All's one. Good faith, how foolish are our minds!

If I do die before thee, prithee, shroud me

In one of those same sheets.

EMILIA.

Come, come, you talk.

DESDEMONA.

My mother had a maid call'd Barbary,

She was in love, and he she lov'd prov'd mad

And did forsake her. She had a song of "willow",

An old thing 'twas, but it express'd her fortune,

And she died singing it. That song tonight

Will not go from my mind. I have much to do

But to go hang my head all at one side

And sing it like poor Barbary. Prithee dispatch.

EMILIA.

Shall I go fetch your night-gown?

DESDEMONA.

No, unpin me here.

This Lodovico is a proper man.

EMILIA.

A very handsome man.

DESDEMONA.

He speaks well.

EMILIA.

I know a lady in Venice would have walked barefoot to Palestine for a touch of his nether lip.

DESDEMONA.

[Singing.]

The poor soul sat sighing by a sycamore tree,

    Sing all a green willow.

Her hand on her bosom, her head on her knee,

    Sing willow, willow, willow.

The fresh streams ran by her, and murmur'd her moans,

    Sing willow, willow, willow;

Her salt tears fell from her, and soften'd the stones;—

Lay by these:—

                                                   [Sings.]

    Sing willow, willow, willow.

Prithee hie thee. He'll come anon.

                                                   [Sings.]

    Sing all a green willow must be my garland.

Let nobody blame him, his scorn I approve,—

Nay, that's not next. Hark! who is't that knocks?

EMILIA.

It's the wind.

DESDEMONA.

                                                   [Sings.]

I call'd my love false love; but what said he then?

    Sing willow, willow, willow:

If I court mo women, you'll couch with mo men.

So get thee gone; good night. Mine eyes do itch;

Doth that bode weeping?

EMILIA.

'Tis neither here nor there.

DESDEMONA.

I have heard it said so. O, these men, these men!

Dost thou in conscience think,—tell me, Emilia,—

That there be women do abuse their husbands

In such gross kind?

EMILIA.

There be some such, no question.

DESDEMONA.

Wouldst thou do such a deed for all the world?

EMILIA.

Why, would not you?

DESDEMONA.

No, by this heavenly light!

EMILIA.

Nor I neither by this heavenly light,

I might do't as well i' the dark.

DESDEMONA.

Wouldst thou do such a deed for all the world?

EMILIA.

The world's a huge thing. It is a great price

For a small vice.

DESDEMONA.

In troth, I think thou wouldst not.

EMILIA.

In troth, I think I should, and undo't when I had done. Marry, I would not do such a thing for a joint-ring, nor for measures of lawn, nor for gowns, petticoats, nor caps, nor any petty exhibition; but, for the whole world—why, who would not make her husband a cuckold to make him a monarch? I should venture purgatory for 't.

DESDEMONA.

Beshrew me, if I would do such a wrong for the whole world.

EMILIA.

Why, the wrong is but a wrong i' the world; and having the world for your labour, 'tis a wrong in your own world, and you might quickly make it right.

DESDEMONA.

I do not think there is any such woman.

EMILIA.

Yes, a dozen; and as many to the vantage as would store the world they played for.

But I do think it is their husbands' faults

If wives do fall: say that they slack their duties,

And pour our treasures into foreign laps;

Or else break out in peevish jealousies,

Throwing restraint upon us. Or say they strike us,

Or scant our former having in despite.

Why, we have galls; and though we have some grace,

Yet have we some revenge. Let husbands know

Their wives have sense like them: they see, and smell

And have their palates both for sweet and sour,

As husbands have. What is it that they do

When they change us for others? Is it sport?

I think it is. And doth affection breed it?

I think it doth. Is't frailty that thus errs?

It is so too. And have not we affections,

Desires for sport, and frailty, as men have?

Then let them use us well: else let them know,

The ills we do, their ills instruct us so.

DESDEMONA.

Good night, good night. Heaven me such usage send,

Not to pick bad from bad, but by bad mend!

[Exeunt.]

ACT V

SCENE I. Cyprus. A Street.

Enter Iago and Roderigo.

IAGO.

Here, stand behind this bulk. Straight will he come.

Wear thy good rapier bare, and put it home.

Quick, quick, fear nothing; I'll be at thy elbow.

It makes us, or it mars us, think on that,

And fix most firm thy resolution.

RODERIGO.

Be near at hand, I may miscarry in 't.

IAGO.

Here, at thy hand. Be bold, and take thy stand.

[Retires to a little distance.]

RODERIGO.

I have no great devotion to the deed;

And yet he hath given me satisfying reasons.

'Tis but a man gone. Forth, my sword; he dies.

[Goes to his stand.]

IAGO.

I have rubb'd this young quat almost to the sense,

And he grows angry. Now, whether he kill Cassio,

Or Cassio him, or each do kill the other,

Every way makes my gain. Live Roderigo,

He calls me to a restitution large

Of gold and jewels that I bobb'd from him,

As gifts to Desdemona.

It must not be. If Cassio do remain,

He hath a daily beauty in his life

That makes me ugly. And besides, the Moor

May unfold me to him; there stand I in much peril.

No, he must die. But so, I hear him coming.

Enter Cassio.

RODERIGO.

I know his gait; 'tis he. Villain, thou diest!

[Rushes out, and makes a pass at Cassio.]

CASSIO.

That thrust had been mine enemy indeed,

But that my coat is better than thou know'st.

I will make proof of thine.

[Draws, and wounds Roderigo.]

RODERIGO.

O, I am slain!

[Iago rushes from his post, cuts Cassio behind in the leg, and exit.]

CASSIO.

I am maim'd forever. Help, ho! murder, murder!

[Falls.]

Enter Othello.

OTHELLO.

The voice of Cassio. Iago keeps his word.

RODERIGO.

O, villain that I am!

OTHELLO.

It is even so.

CASSIO.

O, help, ho! light! a surgeon!

OTHELLO.

'Tis he. O brave Iago, honest and just,

That hast such noble sense of thy friend's wrong!

Thou teachest me,—minion, your dear lies dead,

And your unbless'd fate hies. Strumpet, I come!

Forth of my heart those charms, thine eyes, are blotted;

Thy bed, lust-stain'd, shall with lust's blood be spotted.

[Exit.]

Enter Lodovico and Gratiano.

CASSIO.

What, ho! No watch? No passage? murder, murder!

GRATIANO.

'Tis some mischance; the cry is very direful.

CASSIO.

O, help!

LODOVICO.

Hark!

RODERIGO.

O wretched villain!

LODOVICO.

Two or three groan. It is a heavy night.

These may be counterfeits. Let's think't unsafe

To come in to the cry without more help.

RODERIGO.

Nobody come? Then shall I bleed to death.

Enter Iago with a light.

LODOVICO.

Hark!

GRATIANO.

Here's one comes in his shirt, with light and weapons.

IAGO.

Who's there? Whose noise is this that cries on murder?

LODOVICO.

We do not know.

IAGO.

Did not you hear a cry?

CASSIO.

Here, here! for heaven's sake, help me!

IAGO.

What's the matter?

GRATIANO.

This is Othello's ancient, as I take it.

LODOVICO.

The same indeed, a very valiant fellow.

IAGO.

What are you here that cry so grievously?

CASSIO.

Iago? O, I am spoil'd, undone by villains!

Give me some help.

IAGO.

O me, lieutenant! What villains have done this?

CASSIO.

I think that one of them is hereabout,

And cannot make away.

IAGO.

O treacherous villains!

[To Lodovico and Gratiano.] What are you there?

Come in and give some help.

RODERIGO.

O, help me here!

CASSIO.

That's one of them.

IAGO.

O murderous slave! O villain!

[Stabs Roderigo.]

RODERIGO.

O damn'd Iago! O inhuman dog!

IAGO.

Kill men i' the dark! Where be these bloody thieves?

How silent is this town! Ho! murder! murder!

What may you be? Are you of good or evil?

LODOVICO.

As you shall prove us, praise us.

IAGO.

Signior Lodovico?

LODOVICO.

He, sir.

IAGO.

I cry you mercy. Here's Cassio hurt by villains.

GRATIANO.

Cassio!

IAGO.

How is't, brother?

CASSIO.

My leg is cut in two.

IAGO.

Marry, heaven forbid!

Light, gentlemen, I'll bind it with my shirt.

Enter Bianca.

BIANCA.

What is the matter, ho? Who is't that cried?

IAGO.

Who is't that cried?

BIANCA.

O my dear Cassio, my sweet Cassio! O Cassio, Cassio, Cassio!

IAGO.

O notable strumpet! Cassio, may you suspect

Who they should be that have thus mangled you?

CASSIO.

No.

GRATIANO.

I am sorry to find you thus; I have been to seek you.

IAGO.

Lend me a garter. So.—O, for a chair,

To bear him easily hence!

BIANCA.

Alas, he faints! O Cassio, Cassio, Cassio!

IAGO.

Gentlemen all, I do suspect this trash

To be a party in this injury.

Patience awhile, good Cassio. Come, come;

Lend me a light. Know we this face or no?

Alas, my friend and my dear countryman

Roderigo? No. Yes, sure; O heaven! Roderigo.

GRATIANO.

What, of Venice?

IAGO.

Even he, sir. Did you know him?

GRATIANO.

Know him? Ay.

IAGO.

Signior Gratiano? I cry you gentle pardon.

These bloody accidents must excuse my manners,

That so neglected you.

GRATIANO.

I am glad to see you.

IAGO.

How do you, Cassio? O, a chair, a chair!

GRATIANO.

Roderigo!

IAGO.

He, he, 'tis he.

[A chair brought in.]

O, that's well said; the chair.

Some good man bear him carefully from hence,

I'll fetch the general's surgeon. [To Bianca] For you, mistress,

Save you your labour. He that lies slain here, Cassio,

Was my dear friend. What malice was between you?

CASSIO.

None in the world. Nor do I know the man.

IAGO.

[To Bianca.] What, look you pale?—O, bear him out o' the air.

[Cassio and Roderigo are borne off.]

Stay you, good gentlemen.—Look you pale, mistress?

Do you perceive the gastness of her eye?

Nay, if you stare, we shall hear more anon.

Behold her well. I pray you, look upon her.

Do you see, gentlemen? Nay, guiltiness will speak

Though tongues were out of use.

Enter Emilia.

EMILIA.

'Las, what's the matter? What's the matter, husband?

IAGO.

Cassio hath here been set on in the dark

By Roderigo, and fellows that are 'scap'd.

189

He's almost slain, and Roderigo dead.

EMILIA.

Alas, good gentleman! alas, good Cassio!

IAGO.

This is the fruit of whoring. Prithee, Emilia,

Go know of Cassio where he supp'd tonight.

What, do you shake at that?

BIANCA.

He supp'd at my house, but I therefore shake not.

IAGO.

O, did he so? I charge you go with me.

EMILIA.

Fie, fie upon thee, strumpet!

BIANCA.

I am no strumpet, but of life as honest

As you that thus abuse me.

EMILIA.

As I? Foh! fie upon thee!

IAGO.

Kind gentlemen, let's go see poor Cassio dress'd.

Come, mistress, you must tell's another tale.

Emilia, run you to the citadel,

And tell my lord and lady what hath happ'd.

Will you go on afore? [Aside.] This is the night

That either makes me or fordoes me quite.

[Exeunt.]

SCENE II. Cyprus. A Bedchamber in the castle.

Desdemona in bed asleep; a light burning.

Enter Othello.

OTHELLO.

It is the cause, it is the cause, my soul,

Let me not name it to you, you chaste stars!

It is the cause. Yet I'll not shed her blood,

Nor scar that whiter skin of hers than snow,

And smooth as monumental alabaster.

Yet she must die, else she'll betray more men.

Put out the light, and then put out the light:

If I quench thee, thou flaming minister,

I can again thy former light restore,

Should I repent me. But once put out thy light,

Thou cunning'st pattern of excelling nature,

I know not where is that Promethean heat

That can thy light relume. When I have pluck'd thy rose,

I cannot give it vital growth again,

It must needs wither. I'll smell it on the tree.

[Kissing her.]

O, balmy breath, that dost almost persuade

Justice to break her sword! One more, one more.

Be thus when thou art dead, and I will kill thee,

And love thee after. One more, and this the last.

So sweet was ne'er so fatal. I must weep,

But they are cruel tears. This sorrow's heavenly,

It strikes where it doth love. She wakes.

DESDEMONA.

Who's there? Othello?

OTHELLO.

Ay, Desdemona.

DESDEMONA.

Will you come to bed, my lord?

OTHELLO.

Have you pray'd tonight, Desdemona?

DESDEMONA.

Ay, my lord.

OTHELLO.

If you bethink yourself of any crime

Unreconcil'd as yet to heaven and grace,

Solicit for it straight.

DESDEMONA.

Alack, my lord, what may you mean by that?

OTHELLO.

Well, do it, and be brief, I will walk by.

I would not kill thy unprepared spirit,

No, heaven forfend! I would not kill thy soul.

DESDEMONA.

Talk you of killing?

OTHELLO.

Ay, I do.

DESDEMONA.

Then heaven have mercy on me!

OTHELLO.

Amen, with all my heart!

DESDEMONA.

If you say so, I hope you will not kill me.

OTHELLO.

Hum!

DESDEMONA.

And yet I fear you, for you are fatal then

When your eyes roll so: why I should fear I know not,

Since guiltiness I know not, but yet I feel I fear.

OTHELLO.

Think on thy sins.

DESDEMONA.

They are loves I bear to you.

OTHELLO.

Ay, and for that thou diest.

DESDEMONA.

That death's unnatural that kills for loving.

Alas, why gnaw you so your nether lip?

Some bloody passion shakes your very frame.

These are portents; but yet I hope, I hope,

They do not point on me.

OTHELLO.

Peace, and be still!

DESDEMONA.

I will so. What's the matter?

OTHELLO.

That handkerchief which I so loved and gave thee,

Thou gav'st to Cassio.

DESDEMONA.

No, by my life and soul!

Send for the man and ask him.

OTHELLO.

Sweet soul, take heed, take heed of perjury,

Thou'rt on thy death-bed.

DESDEMONA.

Ay, but not yet to die.

OTHELLO.

Yes, presently:

Therefore confess thee freely of thy sin.

For to deny each article with oath

Cannot remove nor choke the strong conception

That I do groan withal. Thou art to die.

DESDEMONA.

Then, Lord have mercy on me!

OTHELLO.

I say, amen.

DESDEMONA.

And have you mercy too! I never did

Offend you in my life,   never lov'd Cassio

But with such general warranty of heaven

As I might love. I never gave him token.

OTHELLO.

By heaven, I saw my handkerchief in 's hand.

O perjur'd woman, thou dost stone my heart,

And mak'st me call what I intend to do

A murder, which I thought a sacrifice.

I saw the handkerchief.

DESDEMONA.

He found it then.

I never gave it him. Send for him hither.

Let him confess a truth.

OTHELLO.

He hath confess'd.

DESDEMONA.

What, my lord?

OTHELLO.

That he hath us'd thee.

DESDEMONA.

How? Unlawfully?

OTHELLO.

Ay.

DESDEMONA.

He will not say so.

OTHELLO.

No, his mouth is stopp'd.

Honest Iago hath ta'en order for 't.

DESDEMONA.

O, my fear interprets! What, is he dead?

OTHELLO.

Had all his hairs been lives, my great revenge

Had stomach for them all.

DESDEMONA.

Alas, he is betray'd, and I undone!

OTHELLO.

Out, strumpet! Weep'st thou for him to my face?

DESDEMONA.

O, banish me, my lord, but kill me not!

OTHELLO.

Down, strumpet!

DESDEMONA.

Kill me tomorrow, let me live tonight!

OTHELLO.

Nay, if you strive,—

DESDEMONA.

But half an hour!

OTHELLO.

Being done, there is no pause.

DESDEMONA.

But while I say one prayer!

OTHELLO.

It is too late.

[Smothers her.]

EMILIA.

[Within.] My lord, my lord! what, ho! my lord, my lord!

OTHELLO.

What noise is this? Not dead? Not yet quite dead?

I that am cruel am yet merciful,

I would not have thee linger in thy pain.

So, so.

EMILIA.

[Within.] What, ho! my lord, my lord!

OTHELLO.

Who's there?

EMILIA.

[Within.] O, good my lord, I would speak a word with you!

OTHELLO.

Yes. 'Tis Emilia, by and by. She's dead.

'Tis like she comes to speak of Cassio's death;

The noise was high.—Ha! no more moving?

Still as the grave. Shall she come in? Were't good?

I think she stirs again; no. What's best to do?

If she come in, she'll sure speak to my wife.

My wife! my wife! what wife? I have no wife.

O, insupportable! O heavy hour!

Methinks it should be now a huge eclipse

Of sun and moon, and that the affrighted globe

Should yawn at alteration.

EMILIA.

[Within.] I do beseech you

That I may speak with you, O, good my lord!

OTHELLO.

I had forgot thee: O, come in, Emilia.

Soft, by and by; let me the curtains draw.

Where art thou?

[Unlocks the door.]

Enter Emilia.

What's the matter with thee now?

EMILIA.

O, my good lord, yonder's foul murders done!

OTHELLO.

What, now?

EMILIA.

But now, my lord.

OTHELLO.

It is the very error of the moon,

She comes more nearer earth than she was wont

And makes men mad.

EMILIA.

Cassio, my lord, hath kill'd a young Venetian

Call'd Roderigo.

OTHELLO.

Roderigo kill'd?

And Cassio kill'd?

EMILIA.

No, Cassio is not kill'd.

OTHELLO.

Not Cassio kill'd! Then murder's out of tune,

And sweet revenge grows harsh.

DESDEMONA.

O, falsely, falsely murder'd!

EMILIA.

Alas, what cry is that?

OTHELLO.

That? What?

EMILIA.

Out, and alas! That was my lady's voice.

Help! help, ho! help! O lady, speak again,

Sweet Desdemona! O sweet mistress, speak!

DESDEMONA.

A guiltless death I die.

EMILIA.

O, who hath done this deed?

DESDEMONA.

Nobody; I myself. Farewell.

Commend me to my kind lord. O, farewell!

[She dies.]

OTHELLO.

Why, how should she be murder'd?

EMILIA.

Alas, who knows?

OTHELLO.

You heard her say herself, it was not I.

EMILIA.

She said so. I must needs report the truth.

OTHELLO.

She's like a liar, gone to burning hell.

'Twas I that kill'd her.

EMILIA.

O, the more angel she,

And you the blacker devil!

OTHELLO.

She turn'd to folly, and she was a whore.

EMILIA.

Thou dost belie her, and thou art a devil.

OTHELLO.

She was false as water.

EMILIA.

Thou art rash as fire, to say

That she was false: O, she was heavenly true!

OTHELLO.

Cassio did top her; ask thy husband else.

O, I were damn'd beneath all depth in hell,

But that I did proceed upon just grounds

To this extremity. Thy husband knew it all.

EMILIA.

My husband?

OTHELLO.

Thy husband.

EMILIA.

That she was false to wedlock?

OTHELLO.

Ay, with Cassio. Nay, had she been true,

If heaven would make me such another world

Of one entire and perfect chrysolite,

I'd not have sold her for it.

EMILIA.

My husband?

OTHELLO.

Ay, 'twas he that told me first.

An honest man he is, and hates the slime

That sticks on filthy deeds.

EMILIA.

My husband?

OTHELLO.

What needs this iterance, woman? I say thy husband.

EMILIA.

O mistress, villainy hath made mocks with love!

My husband say that she was false?

OTHELLO.

He, woman;

I say thy husband: dost understand the word?

My friend, thy husband, honest, honest Iago.

EMILIA.

If he say so, may his pernicious soul

Rot half a grain a day! he lies to the heart.

She was too fond of her most filthy bargain.

OTHELLO.

Ha!

EMILIA.

Do thy worst:

This deed of thine is no more worthy heaven

Than thou wast worthy her.

OTHELLO.

Peace, you were best.

EMILIA.

Thou hast not half that power to do me harm

As I have to be hurt. O gull! O dolt!

204

As ignorant as dirt! Thou hast done a deed

(I care not for thy sword) I'll make thee known,

Though I lost twenty lives. Help! help, ho! help!

The Moor hath kill'd my mistress! Murder, murder!

Enter Montano, Gratiano and Iago.

MONTANO.

What is the matter? How now, general?

EMILIA.

O, are you come, Iago? You have done well,

That men must lay their murders on your neck.

GRATIANO.

What is the matter?

EMILIA.

Disprove this villain, if thou be'st a man.

He says thou told'st him that his wife was false.

I know thou didst not, thou'rt not such a villain.

Speak, for my heart is full.

IAGO.

I told him what I thought, and told no more

Than what he found himself was apt and true.

EMILIA.

But did you ever tell him she was false?

IAGO.

I did.

205

EMILIA.

You told a lie, an odious, damned lie;

Upon my soul, a lie; a wicked lie.

She false with Cassio? Did you say with Cassio?

IAGO.

With Cassio, mistress. Go to, charm your tongue.

EMILIA.

I will not charm my tongue; I am bound to speak.

My mistress here lies murder'd in her bed.

ALL.

O heavens forfend!

EMILIA.

And your reports have set the murder on.

OTHELLO.

Nay, stare not, masters, it is true indeed.

GRATIANO.

'Tis a strange truth.

MONTANO.

O monstrous act!

EMILIA.

Villany, villany, villany!

I think upon't, I think I smell't; O villany!

I thought so then. I'll kill myself for grief.

O villany, villany!

IAGO.

What, are you mad? I charge you, get you home.

EMILIA.

Good gentlemen, let me have leave to speak.

'Tis proper I obey him, but not now.

Perchance, Iago, I will ne'er go home.

OTHELLO.

O! O! O!

[Hanging over his wife.]

EMILIA.

Nay, lay thee down and roar;

For thou hast kill'd the sweetest innocent

That e'er did lift up eye.

OTHELLO.

[Rising.] O, she was foul!

I scarce did know you, uncle, there lies your niece,

Whose breath indeed these hands have newly stopp'd.

I know this act shows horrible and grim.

GRATIANO.

Poor Desdemona! I am glad thy father's dead.

Thy match was mortal to him, and pure grief

Shore his old thread in twain: did he live now,

This sight would make him do a desperate turn,

Yea, curse his better angel from his side,

And fall to reprobance.

OTHELLO.

'Tis pitiful. But yet Iago knows

That she with Cassio hath the act of shame

A thousand times committed; Cassio confess'd it,

And she did gratify his amorous works

With that recognizance and pledge of love

Which I first gave her; I saw it in his hand.

It was a handkerchief, an antique token

My father gave my mother.

EMILIA.

O heaven! O heavenly powers!

IAGO.

Come, hold your peace.

EMILIA.

'Twill out, 'twill out. I peace?

No, I will speak as liberal as the north.

Let heaven and men and devils, let them all,

All, all, cry shame against me, yet I'll speak.

IAGO.

Be wise, and get you home.

EMILIA.

I will not.

[Iago offers to stab his wife.]

GRATIANO.

Fie!

Your sword upon a woman?

EMILIA.

O thou dull Moor, that handkerchief thou speak'st of

I found by fortune and did give my husband;

For often with a solemn earnestness,

More than indeed belong'd to such a trifle,

He begg'd of me to steal it.

IAGO.

Villanous whore!

EMILIA.

She give it Cassio! no, alas, I found it,

And I did give't my husband.

IAGO.

Filth, thou liest!

EMILIA.

By heaven, I do not, I do not, gentlemen.

O murderous coxcomb! What should such a fool

Do with so good a wife?

OTHELLO

Are there not stones in heaven

But what serve for thunder? Precious villain!

[Iago stabs Emilia and then runs out.]

GRATIANO.

The woman falls. Sure, he hath kill'd his wife.

EMILIA.

Ay, ay. O, lay me by my mistress' side.

GRATIANO.

He's gone, but his wife's kill'd.

MONTANO.

'Tis a notorious villain. Take you this weapon,

Which I have here recover'd from the Moor.

Come, guard the door without, let him not pass,

But kill him rather. I'll after that same villain,

For 'tis a damned slave.

[Exit Montano and Gratiano.]

OTHELLO.

I am not valiant neither,

But every puny whipster gets my sword.

But why should honour outlive honesty?

Let it go all.

EMILIA.

What did thy song bode, lady?

Hark, canst thou hear me? I will play the swan,

And die in music.

[Sings.] Willow, willow, willow.

Moor, she was chaste. She lov'd thee, cruel Moor,

So come my soul to bliss, as I speak true;

So speaking as I think, I die, I die.

[She dies.]

OTHELLO.

I have another weapon in this chamber,

It is a sword of Spain, the ice-brook's temper.

O, here it is. Uncle, I must come forth.

GRATIANO.

[Within.] If thou attempt it, it will cost thee dear;

Thou hast no weapon, and perforce must suffer.

OTHELLO.

Look in upon me then, and speak with me,

Or, naked as I am, I will assault thee.

Enter Gratiano.

GRATIANO.

What is the matter?

OTHELLO.

Behold, I have a weapon.

A better never did itself sustain

Upon a soldier's thigh: I have seen the day

That with this little arm and this good sword

I have made my way through more impediments

Than twenty times your stop. But, O vain boast!

Who can control his fate? 'Tis not so now.

Be not afraid, though you do see me weapon'd.

Here is my journey's end, here is my butt,

And very sea-mark of my utmost sail.

Do you go back dismay'd? 'Tis a lost fear.

Man but a rush against Othello's breast,

And he retires. Where should Othello go?

Now, how dost thou look now? O ill-starr'd wench,

Pale as thy smock, when we shall meet at compt,

This look of thine will hurl my soul from heaven,

And fiends will snatch at it. Cold, cold, my girl!

Even like thy chastity.

O cursed, cursed slave! Whip me, ye devils,

From the possession of this heavenly sight!

Blow me about in winds, roast me in sulphur,

Wash me in steep-down gulfs of liquid fire!

O Desdemon! Dead, Desdemon! dead! Oh, oh!

Enter Lodovico, Montano, Cassio carried in a chair, and Officers with Iago prisoner.

LODOVICO.

Where is this rash and most unfortunate man?

OTHELLO.

That's he that was Othello. Here I am.

LODOVICO.

Where is that viper? Bring the villain forth.

OTHELLO.

I look down towards his feet; but that's a fable.

If that thou be'st a devil, I cannot kill thee.

[Wounds Iago.]

LODOVICO.

Wrench his sword from him.

IAGO.

I bleed, sir, but not kill'd.

OTHELLO.

I am not sorry neither. I'd have thee live,

For in my sense 'tis happiness to die.

LODOVICO.

O thou Othello, that wert once so good,

Fall'n in the practice of a damned slave,

What shall be said to thee?

OTHELLO.

Why, anything;

An honourable murderer, if you will.

For naught did I in hate, but all in honour.

LODOVICO.

This wretch hath part confess'd his villany.

Did you and he consent in Cassio's death?

OTHELLO.

Ay.

CASSIO.

Dear general, I never gave you cause.

OTHELLO.

I do believe it, and I ask your pardon.

Will you, I pray, demand that demi-devil

Why he hath thus ensnar'd my soul and body?

IAGO.

Demand me nothing. What you know, you know.

From this time forth I never will speak word.

LODOVICO.

What, not to pray?

GRATIANO.

Torments will ope your lips.

OTHELLO.

Well, thou dost best.

LODOVICO.

Sir, you shall understand what hath befall'n,

Which, as I think, you know not. Here is a letter

Found in the pocket of the slain Roderigo,

And here another. The one of them imports

The death of Cassio, to be undertook

By Roderigo.

OTHELLO.

O villain!

CASSIO.

Most heathenish and most gross!

LODOVICO.

Now here's another discontented paper,

Found in his pocket too; and this, it seems,

Roderigo meant to have sent this damned villain,

But that, belike, Iago in the interim

Came in and satisfied him.

OTHELLO.

O the pernicious caitiff!

How came you, Cassio, by that handkerchief

That was my wife's?

CASSIO.

I found it in my chamber.

And he himself confess'd but even now,

That there he dropp'd it for a special purpose

Which wrought to his desire.

OTHELLO.

O fool! fool! fool!

CASSIO.

There is besides in Roderigo's letter,

How he upbraids Iago, that he made him

Brave me upon the watch, whereon it came

That I was cast. And even but now he spake,

After long seeming dead, Iago hurt him,

Iago set him on.

LODOVICO.

You must forsake this room, and go with us.

Your power and your command is taken off,

And Cassio rules in Cyprus. For this slave,

If there be any cunning cruelty

That can torment him much and hold him long,

It shall be his. You shall close prisoner rest,

Till that the nature of your fault be known

To the Venetian state. Come, bring away.

OTHELLO.

Soft you; a word or two before you go.

I have done the state some service, and they know't.

No more of that. I pray you, in your letters,

When you shall these unlucky deeds relate,

Speak of me as I am. Nothing extenuate,

Nor set down aught in malice. Then must you speak

Of one that loved not wisely, but too well;

Of one not easily jealous, but being wrought,

Perplex'd in the extreme; of one whose hand,

Like the base Judean, threw a pearl away

Richer than all his tribe; of one whose subdu'd eyes,

Albeit unused to the melting mood,

Drop tears as fast as the Arabian trees

Their medicinal gum. Set you down this.

And say besides, that in Aleppo once,

Where a malignant and a turban'd Turk

Beat a Venetian and traduc'd the state,

I took by the throat the circumcised dog,

And smote him, thus.

[Stabs himself.]

LODOVICO.

O bloody period!

GRATIANO.

All that's spoke is marr'd.

OTHELLO.

I kiss'd thee ere I kill'd thee. No way but this,

Killing myself, to die upon a kiss.

[Falling upon Desdemona.]

CASSIO.

This did I fear, but thought he had no weapon,

For he was great of heart.

LODOVICO.

[To Iago.] O Spartan dog,

More fell than anguish, hunger, or the sea,

Look on the tragic loading of this bed.

This is thy work. The object poisons sight,

Let it be hid. Gratiano, keep the house,

And seize upon the fortunes of the Moor,

For they succeed on you. To you, lord governor,

Remains the censure of this hellish villain.

The time, the place, the torture, O, enforce it!

Myself will straight aboard, and to the state

This heavy act with heavy heart relate.

[Exeunt.]

About Author

Shakespeare produced most of his known works between 1589 and 1613. His early plays were primarily comedies and histories and are regarded as some of the best work produced in these genres. Until about 1608, he wrote mainly tragedies, among them Hamlet, Othello, King Lear, and Macbeth, all considered to be among the finest works in the English language. In the last phase of his life, he wrote tragicomedies (also known as romances) and collaborated with other playwrights.

Many of Shakespeare's plays were published in editions of varying quality and accuracy in his lifetime. However, in 1623, two fellow actors and friends of Shakespeare's, John Heminges and Henry Condell, published a more definitive text known as the First Folio, a posthumous collected edition of Shakespeare's dramatic works that included all but two of his plays. The volume was prefaced with a poem by Ben Jonson, in which Jonson presciently hails Shakespeare in a now-famous quote as "not of an age, but for all time".

Throughout the 20th and 21st centuries, Shakespeare's works have been continually adapted and rediscovered by new movements in scholarship and performance. His plays remain popular and are studied, performed, and reinterpreted through various cultural and political contexts around the world.

Early life

William Shakespeare was the son of John Shakespeare, an alderman and a successful glover (glove-maker) originally from Snitterfield, and Mary Arden, the daughter of an affluent landowning farmer. He was born in Stratford-upon-Avon and baptised there on 26 April 1564. His actual date of birth remains unknown, but is traditionally observed on 23 April, Saint George's Day. This date, which can be traced to a mistake made by an 18th-century scholar, has proved appealing to biographers because Shakespeare died on the same date in 1616. He was the third of eight children, and the eldest surviving son.

Although no attendance records for the period survive, most biographers agree that Shakespeare was probably educated at the King's New School in Stratford, a free school chartered in 1553, about a quarter-mile (400 m) from his home. Grammar schools varied in quality during the Elizabethan era, but grammar school curricula were largely similar: the basic Latin text was standardised by royal decree, and the school would have provided an intensive education in grammar based upon Latin classical authors.

At the age of 18, Shakespeare married 26-year-old Anne Hathaway. The consistory court of the Diocese of Worcester issued a marriage licence on 27 November 1582. The next day, two of Hathaway's neighbours posted bonds guaranteeing that no lawful claims impeded the marriage. The ceremony may have been arranged in some haste since the Worcester chancellor allowed the marriage banns to be read once instead of the usual three times, and six months after the marriage Anne gave birth to a daughter, Susanna, baptised 26 May 1583. Twins, son Hamnet and daughter Judith, followed almost two years later and were baptised 2 February 1585. Hamnet died of unknown causes at the age of 11 and was buried 11 August 1596.

After the birth of the twins, Shakespeare left few historical traces until he is mentioned as part of the London theatre scene in 1592. The exception is the appearance of his name in the "complaints bill" of a law case before the Queen's Bench court at Westminster dated Michaelmas Term 1588 and 9 October 1589. Scholars refer to the years between 1585 and 1592 as Shakespeare's "lost years". Biographers attempting to account for this period have reported many apocryphal stories. Nicholas Rowe, Shakespeare's first biographer, recounted a Stratford legend that Shakespeare fled the town for London to escape prosecution for deer poaching in the estate of local squire Thomas Lucy. Shakespeare is also supposed to have taken his revenge on Lucy by writing a scurrilous ballad about him. Another 18th-century story has Shakespeare starting his theatrical career minding the horses of theatre patrons in London. John Aubrey reported that Shakespeare had been a country schoolmaster. Some 20th-century scholars have suggested that Shakespeare may have been employed as a schoolmaster by Alexander

Hoghton of Lancashire, a Catholic landowner who named a certain "William Shakeshafte" in his will. Little evidence substantiates such stories other than hearsay collected after his death, and Shakeshafte was a common name in the Lancashire area.

London and theatrical career

It is not known definitively when Shakespeare began writing, but contemporary allusions and records of performances show that several of his plays were on the London stage by 1592. By then, he was sufficiently known in London to be attacked in print by the playwright Robert Greene in his Groats-Worth of Wit:

... there is an upstart Crow, beautified with our feathers, that with his Tiger's heart wrapped in a Player's hide, supposes he is as well able to bombast out a blank verse as the best of you: and being an absolute Johannes factotum, is in his own conceit the only Shake-scene in a country.

Scholars differ on the exact meaning of Greene's words, but most agree that Greene was accusing Shakespeare of reaching above his rank in trying to match such university-educated writers as Christopher Marlowe, Thomas Nashe, and Greene himself (the so-called "University Wits"). The italicised phrase parodying the line "Oh, tiger's heart wrapped in a woman's hide" from Shakespeare's Henry VI, Part 3, along with the pun "Shake-scene", clearly identify Shakespeare as Greene's target. As used here, Johannes Factotum ("Jack of all trades") refers to a second-rate tinkerer with the work of others, rather than the more common "universal genius".

Greene's attack is the earliest surviving mention of Shakespeare's work in the theatre. Biographers suggest that his career may have begun any time from the mid-1580s to just before Greene's remarks. After 1594, Shakespeare's plays were performed only by the Lord Chamberlain's Men, a company owned by a group of players, including Shakespeare, that soon became the leading playing company in London. After the death of Queen Elizabeth in 1603, the company was awarded a royal patent by the new King James I, and changed its name to the King's Men.

"All the world's a stage,

and all the men and women merely players:

they have their exits and their entrances;

and one man in his time plays many parts ..."

—As You Like It, Act II, Scene 7, 139–142

In 1599, a partnership of members of the company built their own theatre on the south bank of the River Thames, which they named the Globe. In 1608, the partnership also took over the Blackfriars indoor theatre. Extant records of Shakespeare's property purchases and investments indicate that his association with the company made him a wealthy man, and in 1597, he bought the second-largest house in Stratford, New Place, and in 1605, invested in a share of the parish tithes in Stratford.

Some of Shakespeare's plays were published in quarto editions, beginning in 1594, and by 1598, his name had become a selling point and began to appear on the title pages. Shakespeare continued to act in his own and other plays after his success as a playwright. The 1616 edition of Ben Jonson's Works names him on the cast lists for Every Man in His Humour (1598) and Sejanus His Fall (1603). The absence of his name from the 1605 cast list for Jonson's Volpone is taken by some scholars as a sign that his acting career was nearing its end. The First Folio of 1623, however, lists Shakespeare as one of "the Principal Actors in all these Plays", some of which were first staged after Volpone, although we cannot know for certain which roles he played. In 1610, John Davies of Hereford wrote that "good Will" played "kingly" roles. In 1709, Rowe passed down a tradition that Shakespeare played the ghost of Hamlet's father. Later traditions maintain that he also played Adam in As You Like It, and the Chorus in Henry V, though scholars doubt the sources of that information.

Throughout his career, Shakespeare divided his time between London and Stratford. In 1596, the year before he bought New Place as his family home in Stratford, Shakespeare was living in the parish of St. Helen's, Bishopsgate, north of the River Thames. He moved across the river to Southwark by 1599, the same year his company constructed the Globe Theatre there. By 1604, he had moved north of the river again, to an area north of St Paul's Cathedral with many fine houses. There, he rented rooms from a French Huguenot named Christopher Mountjoy, a maker of ladies' wigs and other headgear.

Later years and death

Rowe was the first biographer to record the tradition, repeated by Johnson, that Shakespeare retired to Stratford "some years before his death". He was still working as an actor in London in 1608; in an answer to the sharers' petition in 1635, Cuthbert Burbage stated that after purchasing the lease of the Blackfriars Theatre in 1608 from Henry Evans, the King's Men "placed men players" there, "which were Heminges, Condell, Shakespeare, etc.". However, it is perhaps relevant that the bubonic plague raged in London throughout 1609. The London public playhouses were repeatedly closed during extended outbreaks of the plague (a total of over 60 months closure between May 1603 and February 1610), which meant there was often no acting work. Retirement from all work was uncommon at that time. Shakespeare continued to visit London during the years 1611–1614. In 1612, he was called as a witness in Bellott v. Mountjoy, a court case concerning the marriage settlement of Mountjoy's daughter, Mary. In March 1613, he bought a gatehouse in the former Blackfriars priory; and from November 1614, he was in London for several weeks with his son-in-law, John Hall. After 1610, Shakespeare wrote fewer plays, and none are attributed to him after 1613. His last three plays were collaborations, probably with John Fletcher, who succeeded him as the house playwright of the King's Men.

Shakespeare died on 23 April 1616, at the age of 52. He died within a month of signing his will, a document which he begins by describing himself as being in "perfect health". No extant contemporary source explains how or why he died. Half a century later, John Ward, the vicar of Stratford, wrote in his notebook: "Shakespeare, Drayton, and Ben Jonson had a merry meeting and, it seems, drank too hard, for Shakespeare died of a fever there contracted", not an impossible scenario since Shakespeare knew Jonson and Drayton. Of the tributes from fellow authors, one refers to his relatively sudden death: "We wondered, Shakespeare, that thou went'st so soon / From

225

the world's stage to the grave's tiring room."

He was survived by his wife and two daughters. Susanna had married a physician, John Hall, in 1607, and Judith had married Thomas Quiney, a vintner, two months before Shakespeare's death. Shakespeare signed his last will and testament on 25 March 1616; the following day, his new son-in-law, Thomas Quiney was found guilty of fathering an illegitimate son by Margaret Wheeler, who had died during childbirth. Thomas was ordered by the church court to do public penance, which would have caused much shame and embarrassment for the Shakespeare family.

Shakespeare bequeathed the bulk of his large estate to his elder daughter Susanna under stipulations that she pass it down intact to "the first son of her body". The Quineys had three children, all of whom died without marrying. The Halls had one child, Elizabeth, who married twice but died without children in 1670, ending Shakespeare's direct line. Shakespeare's will scarcely mentions his wife, Anne, who was probably entitled to one-third of his estate automatically. He did make a point, however, of leaving her "my second best bed", a bequest that has led to much speculation. Some scholars see the bequest as an insult to Anne, whereas others believe that the second-best bed would have been the matrimonial bed and therefore rich in significance.

Shakespeare was buried in the chancel of the Holy Trinity Church two days after his death. The epitaph carved into the stone slab covering his grave includes a curse against moving his bones, which was carefully avoided during restoration of the church in 2008:

Good frend for Iesvs sake forbeare,

To digg the dvst encloased heare.

Bleste be Middle English the.svg man Middle English that.svg spares thes stones,

And cvrst be he Middle English that.svg moves my bones.

(Modern spelling: Good friend, for Jesus' sake forbear, / To dig the dust enclosed here. / Blessed be the man that spares these stones, / And cursed be

226

he that moves my bones.)

Some time before 1623, a funerary monument was erected in his memory on the north wall, with a half-effigy of him in the act of writing. Its plaque compares him to Nestor, Socrates, and Virgil. In 1623, in conjunction with the publication of the First Folio, the Droeshout engraving was published.

Shakespeare has been commemorated in many statues and memorials around the world, including funeral monuments in Southwark Cathedral and Poets' Corner in Westminster Abbey.

Plays

Most playwrights of the period typically collaborated with others at some point, and critics agree that Shakespeare did the same, mostly early and late in his career. Some attributions, such as Titus Andronicus and the early history plays, remain controversial while The Two Noble Kinsmen and the lost Cardenio have well-attested contemporary documentation. Textual evidence also supports the view that several of the plays were revised by other writers after their original composition.

The first recorded works of Shakespeare are Richard III and the three parts of Henry VI, written in the early 1590s during a vogue for historical drama. Shakespeare's plays are difficult to date precisely, however, and studies of the texts suggest that Titus Andronicus, The Comedy of Errors, The Taming of the Shrew, and The Two Gentlemen of Verona may also belong to Shakespeare's earliest period. His first histories, which draw heavily on the 1587 edition of Raphael Holinshed's Chronicles of England, Scotland, and Ireland, dramatise the destructive results of weak or corrupt rule and have been interpreted as a justification for the origins of the Tudor dynasty. The early plays were influenced by the works of other Elizabethan dramatists, especially Thomas Kyd and Christopher Marlowe, by the traditions of medieval drama, and by the plays of Seneca. The Comedy of Errors was also based on classical models, but no source for The Taming of the Shrew has been found, though it is related to a separate play of the same name and may have derived from a folk story. Like The Two Gentlemen of Verona, in which two friends appear to approve of rape, the Shrew's story of the taming of a woman's independent spirit by a man sometimes troubles modern critics, directors, and audiences.

Shakespeare's early classical and Italianate comedies, containing tight double plots and precise comic sequences, give way in the mid-1590s to the romantic atmosphere of his most acclaimed comedies. A Midsummer Night's Dream is a witty mixture of romance, fairy magic, and comic lowlife scenes. Shakespeare's next comedy, the equally romantic Merchant of Venice, contains a portrayal of the vengeful Jewish moneylender Shylock, which reflects Elizabethan views but may appear derogatory to modern audiences. The wit and wordplay of Much Ado About Nothing, the charming rural setting of As You Like It, and the lively merrymaking of Twelfth Night complete Shakespeare's sequence of great comedies. After the lyrical Richard II, written almost entirely in verse, Shakespeare introduced prose comedy into the histories of the late 1590s, Henry IV, parts 1 and 2, and Henry V. His characters become more complex and tender as he switches deftly between comic and serious scenes, prose and poetry, and achieves the narrative variety of his mature work. This period begins and ends with two tragedies: Romeo and Juliet, the famous romantic tragedy of sexually charged adolescence, love, and death; and Julius Caesar—based on Sir Thomas North's 1579 translation of Plutarch's Parallel Lives—which introduced a new kind of drama. According to Shakespearean scholar James Shapiro, in Julius Caesar, "the various strands of politics, character, inwardness, contemporary events, even Shakespeare's own reflections on the act of writing, began to infuse each other".

In the early 17th century, Shakespeare wrote the so-called "problem plays" Measure for Measure, Troilus and Cressida, and All's Well That Ends Well and a number of his best known tragedies. Many critics believe that Shakespeare's greatest tragedies represent the peak of his art. The titular hero of one of Shakespeare's greatest tragedies, Hamlet, has probably been discussed more than any other Shakespearean character, especially for his famous soliloquy which begins "To be or not to be; that is the question". Unlike the introverted Hamlet, whose fatal flaw is hesitation, the heroes of the tragedies that followed, Othello and King Lear, are undone by hasty errors of judgement. The plots of Shakespeare's tragedies often hinge on such fatal errors or flaws, which overturn order and destroy the hero and those he loves. In Othello, the villain Iago stokes Othello's sexual jealousy to the point where he murders the innocent wife who loves him. In King Lear, the old king commits the tragic error of giving up his powers, initiating the events which lead to the torture and blinding of the Earl of Gloucester and the murder of Lear's youngest daughter Cordelia. According to the critic Frank Kermode, "the play-offers neither its good characters nor its audience any relief from its cruelty". In Macbeth, the shortest and most compressed of Shakespeare's tragedies, uncontrollable ambition incites Macbeth and his wife, Lady Macbeth, to murder the rightful king and usurp the throne until their own guilt destroys them in turn. In this play, Shakespeare adds a supernatural element to the tragic structure. His last major tragedies, Antony and Cleopatra and Coriolanus, contain some of Shakespeare's finest poetry and were considered his most successful tragedies by the poet and critic T.S. Eliot.

In his final period, Shakespeare turned to romance or tragicomedy and completed three more major plays: Cymbeline, The Winter's Tale, and The Tempest, as well as the collaboration, Pericles, Prince of Tyre. Less bleak than the tragedies, these four plays are graver in tone than the comedies of the 1590s, but they end with reconciliation and the forgiveness of potentially tragic errors. Some commentators have seen this change in mood as evidence of a more serene view of life on Shakespeare's part, but it may merely reflect the theatrical fashion of the day. Shakespeare collaborated on two further surviving plays, Henry VIII and The Two Noble Kinsmen, probably with John Fletcher.

Performances

It is not clear for which companies Shakespeare wrote his early plays. The title page of the 1594 edition of Titus Andronicus reveals that the play had been acted by three different troupes. After the plagues of 1592–3, Shakespeare's plays were performed by his own company at The Theatre and the Curtain in Shoreditch, north of the Thames. Londoners flocked there to see the first part of Henry IV, Leonard Digges recording, "Let but Falstaff come, Hal, Poins, the rest ... and you scarce shall have a room". When the company found themselves in dispute with their landlord, they pulled The

Theatre down and used the timbers to construct the Globe Theatre, the first playhouse built by actors for actors, on the south bank of the Thames at Southwark. The Globe opened in autumn 1599, with Julius Caesar one of the first plays staged. Most of Shakespeare's greatest post-1599 plays were written for the Globe, including Hamlet, Othello, and King Lear.

After the Lord Chamberlain's Men were renamed the King's Men in 1603, they entered a special relationship with the new King James. Although the performance records are patchy, the King's Men performed seven of Shakespeare's plays at court between 1 November 1604, and 31 October 1605, including two performances of The Merchant of Venice. After 1608, they performed at the indoor Blackfriars Theatre during the winter and the Globe during the summer. The indoor setting, combined with the Jacobean fashion for lavishly staged masques, allowed Shakespeare to introduce more elaborate stage devices. In Cymbeline, for example, Jupiter descends "in thunder and lightning, sitting upon an eagle: he throws a thunderbolt. The ghosts fall on their knees."

The actors in Shakespeare's company included the famous Richard Burbage, William Kempe, Henry Condell and John Heminges. Burbage played the leading role in the first performances of many of Shakespeare's plays, including Richard III, Hamlet, Othello, and King Lear. The popular comic actor Will Kempe played the servant Peter in Romeo and Juliet and Dogberry in Much Ado About Nothing, among other characters. He was replaced around 1600 by Robert Armin, who played roles such as Touchstone in As You Like It and the fool in King Lear. In 1613, Sir Henry Wotton recorded that Henry VIII "was set forth with many extraordinary circumstances of pomp and ceremony". On 29 June, however, a cannon set fire to the thatch of the Globe and burned the theatre to the ground, an event which pinpoints the date of a Shakespeare play with rare precision.

Textual sources

In 1623, John Heminges and Henry Condell, two of Shakespeare's friends from the King's Men, published the First Folio, a collected edition of Shakespeare's plays. It contained 36 texts, including 18 printed for the first time. Many of the plays had already appeared in quarto versions—flimsy books made from sheets of paper folded twice to make four leaves. No evidence suggests that Shakespeare approved these editions, which the First Folio describes as "stol'n and surreptitious copies". Nor did Shakespeare plan or expect his works to survive in any form at all; those works likely would have faded into oblivion but for his friends' spontaneous idea, after his death, to create and publish the First Folio.

Alfred Pollard termed some of the pre-1623 versions as "bad quartos" because of their adapted, paraphrased or garbled texts, which may in places have been reconstructed from memory. Where several versions of a play survive, each differs from the other. The differences may stem from copying or printing errors, from notes by actors or audience members, or from Shakespeare's own papers. In some cases, for example, Hamlet, Troilus and Cressida, and Othello, Shakespeare could have revised the texts between the quarto and folio editions. In the case of King Lear, however, while most modern editions do conflate them, the 1623 folio version is so different from the 1608 quarto that the Oxford Shakespeare prints them both, arguing that they cannot be conflated without confusion.

Influence from neighbours in London

Ten years of research by Geoffrey Marsh (museum director) of the Victoria and Albert Museum in London may have shown that Shakespeare got many of the ideas and information for his plays, from his neighbours that he lived near in London in the late 1590s.

Geoffrey Marsh found the site of Shakespeare's house in St Helen's Church, Bishopsgate parish, at the corner of St.Helen's churchyard and Bishopsgate Street, north of the churchyard, from the records of the Leathersellers Company. Many wealthy and notable people (including Sir John Spencer and Dr. Edward Jorden and Dr. Peter Turner), with connections across Europe, lived near Shakespeare.

Poems

In 1593 and 1594, when the theatres were closed because of plague,

Shakespeare published two narrative poems on sexual themes, Venus and Adonis and The Rape of Lucrece. He dedicated them to Henry Wriothesley, Earl of Southampton. In Venus and Adonis, an innocent Adonis rejects the sexual advances of Venus; while in The Rape of Lucrece, the virtuous wife Lucrece is raped by the lustful Tarquin. Influenced by Ovid's Metamorphoses, the poems show the guilt and moral confusion that result from uncontrolled lust. Both proved popular and were often reprinted during Shakespeare's lifetime. A third narrative poem, A Lover's Complaint, in which a young woman laments her seduction by a persuasive suitor, was printed in the first edition of the Sonnets in 1609. Most scholars now accept that Shakespeare wrote A Lover's Complaint. Critics consider that its fine qualities are marred by leaden effects. The Phoenix and the Turtle, printed in Robert Chester's 1601 Love's Martyr, mourns the deaths of the legendary phoenix and his lover, the faithful turtle dove. In 1599, two early drafts of sonnets 138 and 144 appeared in The Passionate Pilgrim, published under Shakespeare's name but without his permission.

Sonnets

Published in 1609, the Sonnets were the last of Shakespeare's non-dramatic works to be printed. Scholars are not certain when each of the 154 sonnets was composed, but evidence suggests that Shakespeare wrote sonnets throughout his career for a private readership. Even before the two unauthorised sonnets appeared in The Passionate Pilgrim in 1599, Francis Meres had referred in 1598 to Shakespeare's "sugred Sonnets among his private friends". Few analysts believe that the published collection follows Shakespeare's intended sequence. He seems to have planned two contrasting series: one about uncontrollable lust for a married woman of dark complexion (the "dark lady"), and one about conflicted love for a fair young man (the "fair youth"). It remains unclear if these figures represent real individuals, or if the authorial "I" who addresses them represents Shakespeare himself, though Wordsworth believed that with the sonnets "Shakespeare unlocked his heart".

"Shall I compare thee to a summer's day?

Thou art more lovely and more temperate ..."

232

—Lines from Shakespeare's Sonnet 18.

The 1609 edition was dedicated to a "Mr. W.H.", credited as "the only begetter" of the poems. It is not known whether this was written by Shakespeare himself or by the publisher, Thomas Thorpe, whose initials appear at the foot of the dedication page; nor is it known who Mr. W.H. was, despite numerous theories, or whether Shakespeare even authorised the publication. Critics praise the Sonnets as a profound meditation on the nature of love, sexual passion, procreation, death, and time.

Style

Shakespeare's first plays were written in the conventional style of the day. He wrote them in a stylised language that does not always spring naturally from the needs of the characters or the drama. The poetry depends on extended, sometimes elaborate metaphors and conceits, and the language is often rhetorical—written for actors to declaim rather than speak. The grand speeches in Titus Andronicus, in the view of some critics, often hold up the action, for example; and the verse in The Two Gentlemen of Verona has been described as stilted.

However, Shakespeare soon began to adapt the traditional styles to his own purposes. The opening soliloquy of Richard III has its roots in the self-declaration of Vice in medieval drama. At the same time, Richard's vivid self-awareness looks forward to the soliloquies of Shakespeare's mature plays. No single play marks a change from the traditional to the freer style. Shakespeare combined the two throughout his career, with Romeo and Juliet perhaps the best example of the mixing of the styles. By the time of Romeo and Juliet, Richard II, and A Midsummer Night's Dream in the mid-1590s, Shakespeare had begun to write a more natural poetry. He increasingly tuned his metaphors and images to the needs of the drama itself.

Shakespeare's standard poetic form was blank verse, composed in iambic pentameter. In practice, this meant that his verse was usually unrhymed and consisted of ten syllables to a line, spoken with a stress on every second syllable. The blank verse of his early plays is quite different from that of his later ones. It is often beautiful, but its sentences tend to start, pause, and finish at the end of lines, with the risk of monotony. Once Shakespeare mastered traditional blank verse, he began to interrupt and vary its flow. This technique releases the new power and flexibility of the poetry in plays such as Julius Caesar and Hamlet. Shakespeare uses it, for example, to convey the turmoil in Hamlet's mind:

> Sir, in my heart there was a kind of fighting
>
> That would not let me sleep. Methought I lay
>
> Worse than the mutines in the bilboes. Rashly—
>
> And prais'd be rashness for it—let us know
>
> Our indiscretion sometimes serves us well ...
>
> —Hamlet, Act 5, Scene 2, 4–8

After Hamlet, Shakespeare varied his poetic style further, particularly in the more emotional passages of the late tragedies. The literary critic A. C. Bradley described this style as "more concentrated, rapid, varied, and, in construction, less regular, not seldom twisted or elliptical". In the last phase of his career, Shakespeare adopted many techniques to achieve these effects. These included run-on lines, irregular pauses and stops, and extreme variations in sentence structure and length. In Macbeth, for example, the language darts from one unrelated metaphor or simile to another: "was the hope drunk/ Wherein you dressed yourself?" (1.7.35–38); "... pity, like a naked new-born babe/ Striding the blast, or heaven's cherubim, hors'd/ Upon the sightless couriers of the air ..." (1.7.21–25). The listener is challenged to complete the sense. The late romances, with their shifts in time and surprising turns of plot, inspired a last poetic style in which long and short sentences are set against one another, clauses are piled up, subject and object are reversed, and words are omitted, creating an effect of spontaneity.

Shakespeare combined poetic genius with a practical sense of the theatre. Like all playwrights of the time, he dramatised stories from sources such as Plutarch and Holinshed. He reshaped each plot to create several centres of interest and to show as many sides of a narrative to the audience as possible. This strength of design ensures that a Shakespeare play can survive translation, cutting and wide interpretation without loss to its core drama. As Shakespeare's mastery grew, he gave his characters clearer and more varied motivations and distinctive patterns of speech. He preserved aspects of his earlier style in the later plays, however. In Shakespeare's late romances, he deliberately returned to a more artificial style, which emphasised the illusion of theatre.

Influence

Shakespeare's work has made a lasting impression on later theatre and literature. In particular, he expanded the dramatic potential of characterisation, plot, language, and genre. Until Romeo and Juliet, for example, romance had not been viewed as a worthy topic for tragedy. Soliloquies had been used mainly to convey information about characters or events, but Shakespeare used them to explore characters' minds. His work heavily influenced later poetry. The Romantic poets attempted to revive Shakespearean verse drama, though with little success. Critic George Steiner described all English verse dramas from Coleridge to Tennyson as "feeble variations on Shakespearean themes."

Shakespeare influenced novelists such as Thomas Hardy, William Faulkner, and Charles Dickens. The American novelist Herman Melville's soliloquies owe much to Shakespeare; his Captain Ahab in Moby-Dick is a classic tragic hero, inspired by King Lear. Scholars have identified 20,000 pieces of music linked to Shakespeare's works. These include three operas by Giuseppe Verdi, Macbeth, Otello and Falstaff, whose critical standing compares with that of the source plays. Shakespeare has also inspired many painters, including the Romantics and the Pre-Raphaelites. The Swiss Romantic artist Henry Fuseli, a friend of William Blake, even translated Macbeth into German. The psychoanalyst Sigmund Freud drew on Shakespearean psychology, in particular, that of Hamlet, for his theories of human nature.

In Shakespeare's day, English grammar, spelling, and pronunciation were less standardised than they are now, and his use of language helped shape modern English. Samuel Johnson quoted him more often than any other author in his A Dictionary of the English Language, the first serious work of its type. Expressions such as "with bated breath" (Merchant of Venice) and "a foregone conclusion" (Othello) have found their way into everyday English speech.

Works

Classification of the plays

Shakespeare's works include the 36 plays printed in the First Folio of 1623, listed according to their folio classification as comedies, histories, and tragedies. Two plays not included in the First Folio, The Two Noble Kinsmen and Pericles, Prince of Tyre, are now accepted as part of the canon, with today's scholars agreeing that Shakespeare made major contributions to the writing of both. No Shakespearean poems were included in the First Folio.

In the late 19th century, Edward Dowden classified four of the late comedies as romances, and though many scholars prefer to call them tragicomedies, Dowden's term is often used. In 1896, Frederick S. Boas coined the term "problem plays" to describe four plays: All's Well That Ends Well, Measure for Measure, Troilus and Cressida, and Hamlet. "Dramas as singular in theme and temper cannot be strictly called comedies or tragedies", he wrote. "We may, therefore, borrow a convenient phrase from the theatre of today and class them together as Shakespeare's problem plays." The term, much debated and sometimes applied to other plays, remains in use, though Hamlet is definitively classed as a tragedy. (Source: Wikipedia)

9 789389 230451